CHASING PICASSO

THE TRUE STORY OF A DAYTIME HEIST ON ART HILL

C. JOAN BAKER

Table of Contents

Preface.. i

Introduction... 1

Chapter 1. The Passing of Two Picassos 11

Chapter 2. Degenerate Art 29

Chapter 3. Swindled Art... 47

Chapter 4. The Enigma of Art Value 57

Chapter 5. A French Secret on Art Hill 75

Chapter 6. The Art of Organized Crime..................... 87

Chapter 7. The Art of Fencing................................... 101

Chapter 8. The Art of the Informant 119

Chapter 9. The Art of Theft & Conspiracy................. 139

Chapter 10. The Pro vs. the Amateur 165

Chapter 11. Where Art Thou, Picasso? 183

Acknowledgments 195

Notes 197

Preface

STORIES OF GREED, MURDER, POWER, AND SORROW seem to follow art crimes. I came to this conclusion after researching the history of art thefts, including a string of art robberies in St. Louis, Missouri, from 1973 to 1978. Of the art stolen in St. Louis from this period, *Nude* was the only significant piece to remain missing. I was convinced few people knew about the dark history of the St. Louis art thefts, but that even fewer knew about the Picasso stolen from the Saint Louis Art Museum in 1973.

The reader doesn't have to be a St. Louis native to appreciate the stories or get in on the chase, as the painting could be anywhere. Mysterious tales loom in just about any art museum. I hope this book inspires others to chase the history behind the art displayed at their local museum. Sometimes the art's past is more provocative than the art itself.

The small oil painting, dubbed *Nude* in news reports of the theft, was also the first significant art theft to defile the museum on Art Hill. For nonlocals, Art Hill is the name of the large slope that descends from the art museum to the Grand Basin, both leftovers from the 1904 World's Fair—the same fair Judy Garland referred to in the song and movie, *Meet Me in St. Louis.*

The museum reported the crime to authorities on April 13, 1973, two days after the theft. The first forty-eight hours after the crime should have been crucial: a chance to interview witnesses and collect physical evidence. In 1973, delaying the report of stolen art was not unusual for a museum. The embarrassment associated with an art theft from a public museum, under the nose of security, was not a flattering reflection of museum leaders.

Picasso's *Nude,* taken from the art museum, is a perfect example of art that went missing from this period in the United States. It was a lesser-known piece of a popular artist, the kind stolen mostly from personal collections, art galleries, and occasionally, art museums. It also would fit into a category of paintings that might not have garnered much publicity.

The publicity of art thefts created two fears for museum directors. First, the news might scare away those who lend their art to museums for display. Second, it might invite more thefts if the security seems inadequate. Yet, as in the case of *Nude,* reporting the story to the news was the only opportunity to share a photo of the stolen art with the public and put pressure on art thieves.

The two major local newspapers, the *St. Louis Globe-Democrat* and the *St. Louis Post-Dispatch,* represented a daily circulation of over 800,000 when the art museum reported the theft. Though the newspaper publicity provided the broadest source of impressions in the local market, it lacked the frequency needed to create a lasting memory.

Paid advertisements featuring the painting, its description, and where to send leads might have been a better tactic if the museum budget supported the effort. Money raised from taxes and donations barely kept the City Art Museum (the former name in 1973) open to the public.

The best chance to bring the painting back to the art museum is to tell the story of the missing Picasso and the circumstances surrounding the art theft. Low awareness of *Nude* and its robbery contributed to it not being recovered over the past half-century.

Two months after *Nude* went missing from the Saint Louis Art Museum, a thief stole a valuable Norman Rockwell painting from a nearby gallery. A string of sporadic thefts continued until 1978, which begged the question: Was *Nude* related to the robberies that followed or an isolated incident?

I attempted to resolve whether a lone opportunist or an organized effort involving multiple figures was to blame for *Nude's* disappearance in 1973. Each possibility offered potentially different outcomes for the painting and its whereabouts.

Aside from entertainment, the ultimate goal of writing the book was to share the mostly forgotten theft so that someone might actually recognize the art and return it to the museum. To do this, I spent over a year researching the art market, art thefts, and St. Louis criminal activity in the 1970s. I had to pay for a license to reproduce the missing painting as his art is copyrighted to the Picasso Estate. Other artworks displayed in this book were courtesy of the Saint Louis Art Museum but converted to black and white to keep the book at a reasonable price.

It was necessary to lean on historical archives and expert sources to recreate the environment that explained how and why *Nude* could have disappeared on April 11, 1973 and remain missing for a half-century. I used my professional research experience to identify and analyze the influences and behaviors that shaped the art market, as well as to explain how art became one of the top criminal trades in the world.

I have no personal ties with the museum, and this is not an authorized biography of the crime or the painting. At times, the story will focus on the details of criminal activity connected to other local art robberies that were central to investigating the forces potentially behind the 1973 theft at the Saint Louis Art Museum.

It became clear that art theft is full of diversified, often dangerous characters, unlike what I saw in films about fictitious heists. Names of public figures and notorious local characters from the period were kept for historical accuracy. However, many characters connected to the St. Louis art thefts, directly or indirectly, were given fictitious names for privacy. They are indicated with an asterisk upon first usage.

The theft of *Nude* is a true story. But the theories I present are my own conclusions based on what I learned through months of research.

Certain characters' and institutions' behaviors were not always clear and required speculation. When it occurs, "maybe, perhaps, possibly, coincidentally," or other similar words indicate an opinion or theory.

Finding new clues about the stolen art from the period was almost an impossible task. *No* internet, *no* art database, and *no* dedicated art investigation team existed in the United States to recover stolen art in 1973. The passing of time led to the legal destruction of any official police or FBI case files of the missing Picasso. Many people involved in these stories have passed, so firsthand accounts were nearly impossible to include.

I was very grateful for the vast digital archives, library microfiche, and various libraries that contained pieces of the puzzle that brought the story of the missing painting back to life.

Old news reports relayed the facts about the thefts soon after they happened; most included eyewitness and law enforcement accounts. The public facts of art theft and crime came from multiple sources when possible; some played out in court cases, others in historical records.

I obtained stories retold in *Chasing Picasso* through credible historical resources; accuracy relies on multiple, consistent references. However, second- and third-hand accounts can be susceptible to errors in memory and reporting. The truth lies with those closest to the events, but most have already taken what they knew to their graves.

Introduction

IT USUALLY SURPRISES others when I mention that St. Louis had a string of art robberies at museums and galleries between 1973 and 1978. The recoveries and the unexpected aftermath were sometimes more shocking than the thefts. The crime wave began with one painting, an outlier compared to the rest that was stolen over those five years. It disappeared from the Saint Louis Art Museum in 1973 and is the only to still be missing. The story behind the disappearance of a Rose Period Picasso was short, quiet, and mostly forgotten. Of all the pieces in this string of art thefts to hit St. Louis, a legal-sized, rectangular oil painting by Pablo Picasso was the most valuable. In 2006, the artwork turned one hundred years old, and in 2023, it will have been missing for fifty years.

Despite its value and the fact it was a Picasso, it might be the least known case of art stolen from any large city museum to ever occur. On April 11, 1973, the Picasso oil painting quietly went out the door under the nose of security guards at the City Art Museum of St. Louis, the previous name of the Saint Louis Art Museum.

Knowledge of the Picasso theft fell into obscurity, a place fitting for this painting. Anonymity plagued its century-old existence, starting with its *provenance*. The provenance is the history of a painting's movement and ownership from the artist to its current owner, which will be discussed in more detail in the chapter addressing its role in assessing value. I will use the term also to discuss the importance of understanding history to detect potential deception in past transactions between owners.

The museum staff must have known little about their new acquisition in 1934. The director dedicated less than a paragraph describing the piece in the October 1934 museum bulletin. The story wrongly attributed the painting's creation to 1907. The bulletin referred to the piece as *A Study of Nude,* which was not the official name of the work. (Though at least more descriptive than *Nude*, the incorrect title spread to the media when it was stolen.) When a museum acquired works of a well-known artist, like Picasso, it would have typically mentioned the art dealer, the most common liaison between the buyer and the seller in the 1930s. The newspaper announcement only described *Nude* as coming from a private collector.

The painting was absent from this period's earliest official catalog of Picasso's art. Picasso worked on this "official" record with its producer, Christian Zervos. Volume 1 covered art from 1895 to 1906, but *Nude* was missing from its pages. The catalog's production started in 1930 and was published in 1932, two years *before* the painting came to the art museum.

Zervos produced a supplemental volume to his earliest period (No. 6) in 1954. *Nude* was still absent from the catalogs, despite being in the city museum collection for two decades.

Two other Picasso historians would finally document the painting in 1967. The Daix and Boudaille catalog focused on art from Picasso's Blue and Rose Periods, 1900 to 1906. This book listed the

City Art Museum of St. Louis as the owner, referencing the museum's October 1934 bulletin in its bibliography. It acknowledged that no listing existed in the official Zervos collection of Picasso works. The title of the painting in the Daix version was *Kneeling Nude Arranging Her Hair*, 1906. This provided one more name and one more date tied to the creation.

Finally, in 1970, *Nude* made it into Zervos's official Picasso reference catalog suite, Volume No. 22, and the third supplement to Volume 1 of Picasso's early work. This version provided only a French title and yet another year: *Nu Agenouillé Se Coiffant*, 1905 (i.e., *Kneeling Nude Combing Her Hair*). It only listed the City Art Museum of St. Louis for its provenance.

Thinking this would be the final word on the official title and year was a wrong assumption. I reached out to the Picasso administration to secure the rights to reproduce the painting in print for the book. The official title and year provided: *Etude pour Femme Agenouillée se Coiffant,* 1906. Translated, *Study for Kneeling Woman Combing Her Hair.*

I came to appreciate the simplicity of *Nude*, despite its lack of accuracy, and used this unofficial title in the book to improve content flow. I was equally thankful to Pablo Diego José Francisco de Paula Juan Nepomuceno Crispín Crispiniano María de los Remedios de la Santísima Trinidad Ruiz Picasso for signing his art and becoming known only as Picasso.

The scholars settled on 1906 as the official year for *Nude* because Picasso featured his mistress, Fernande Olivier, as the model for the painting. He created her likeness in this style for most of his work completed in the summer and fall of 1906. Picasso's style changed in 1907 when he and the artist, Georges Braque, invented Cubism. Cubism put Picasso on the world map, taking him out of impoverishment. By the time Picasso died on April 8, 1973, he was a multimillionaire with a vast estate.

Nude was the first Picasso stolen from any museum after Picasso's death, at least that I could find. The artist was not even in the grave when the painting disappeared.

Picasso's works were plentiful, and even though the oil was a lesser-known work of his Rose Period, the potential value remains significant. Between inflation, compound annual growth rates during the time the museum held the piece, and the value of some of his other Rose Period works, the missing painting could be worth millions.

ART THEFTS

Experts consider the modern art master the most prolific artist ever. According to the Guinness World Records website, "It has been estimated that Picasso produced about 13,500 paintings and designs, 100,000 prints and engravings, 34,000 book illustrations, and 300 sculptures and ceramics." With such a high production rate, it was no wonder his works were the most pilfered of any artist. Somewhere around 1,100 pieces have been lost to thieves.

The most frustrating element of art theft cases for investigators, I imagine, was the ease with which thieves stole art. Art thefts reached an epidemic proportion in France in 1961, and another painting from the City Art Museum collection was lifted while on loan to a French museum. Art values rose and collections remained in unsecure venues. It was an irresistible combination for thieves.

By the late 1960s, widespread art thefts occurred in the United States. Thieves targeted personal art collections more than any other venue. Museums fared better than galleries perhaps because a museum heist was more likely to be publicized than a gallery theft.

Investigators usually cited either monetary gain via a ransom scheme or black market demand for art as the motive behind art thefts. Shady art dealers were commonly referred to as the source of black market sales to wealthy buyers.

Up to this point, movies and our own perceptions shaped the criminal profile of art thieves: they must be the same people who can spend gobs of money on a Picasso, Rembrandt, Leonardo da Vinci, or a piece by some other master artist. Like in *The Thomas Crown Affair*, most people, including investigators, saw stolen art as rich-people problems.

The only people who could afford art were those with plenty of disposable income, so the common belief was that other rich people hired thieves to steal art. The truth was that rich people often lost their art to criminals. The idea of a millionaire mastermind was mostly false and may have delayed the progress in investigating art thefts.

Successful art robberies led to more art crimes, and soon there were too many to investigate. Stolen property favored the criminal, and successful prosecutions were rare events that resulted in short sentences or none at all.

In 1973, law enforcement battled a double-digit growth, year over year, of stateside art thefts, compounding the issue of the stolen Picasso. Pinched art around the world was heading into the US more than any other country. Days before *Nude* was stolen, a national story was released to newspapers across the States listing twelve of the most valuable pieces of art stolen and believed to be circulating within North America's borders.

Interpol called it "Rogues Gallery of Art" and the Washington, DC office planned to make the list public every six months. They circulated the list to art publications, dealers, and museums, with plans to get the public further involved, which may or may not have happened.

However, art thieves evolved their scheme when they began taking popular artists' lesser-known works. This art might not have made the Rogues Gallery list because the art's value ranked lower on the scale of plundered art circulating in the early 1970s.

Investigators often mistook the theft of lesser-valuable objects as signs of amateur thieves. In reality, size mattered in terms of what a thief could physically get away with in a robbery. Nude was vulnerable for theft because it was just 8½ x 14¹⁄₁₆ inches. The most difficult aspect of stealing Nude, however, was that it was painted on wood. It could not be cut and then rolled into a tube for transport like a similar-sized Van Gogh stolen in California four days later. The Picasso had to be placed in a large purse, shopping bag, or slipped into a false pocket of a jacket to make it out of the St. Louis museum.

The theft occurred at a time when art disappeared at a rapid pace. Investigators were still at a loss to understand the types of criminals who contributed to the epidemic of art thefts when *Nude* vanished. The DC bureau's Interpol chief stated from the period, "We don't know where the art traffic pattern is heading or where art goes."

Interpol had no authority to arrest a suspected thief, so they worked with law enforcement within a case's jurisdiction. In the States, the Federal Bureau of Investigation (FBI) and local police handled valuable thefts like *Nude*. Neither had a dedicated art team. The FBI had one person in DC dedicated to art thefts. Considering the FBI did not develop psychological profiles of serial killers until the 1970s, art thief profiles were nowhere in the near future.

The movies glorified art heists and portrayed art thieves as nonviolent and almost antiestablishment heroes. Most art thefts were nonviolent, but violent people usually surrounded the actual crime. An art thief usually did not shoot at security guards during an art heist. They preferred to rob a museum without detection. That did not mean an art thief wasn't willing to kill a partner over the financial split or silence a snitch.

The motive for art theft was not always money, though that was still the most prominent reason for stealing art. Monetary gain was too broad and needed to be broken down into all the potential ways criminals could move stolen art into open and black markets.

The individual opportunist looking to improve their economic status stole art. They could take the art as a future investment to cash in long after publicity subsided. A thief hedging their bet on a jump in value might have quickly reacted to the news of Picasso's death and stolen it.

Another potential motive was art stolen for its intrinsic value. Art can move people emotionally and foster unexpected behaviors. Mourning the loss of the great master could have inspired someone to take the art to own a piece of his legacy.

With the mystery surrounding the painting's provenance, a theft motivated by its past could not be excluded. The museum acquired it during the second year of Hitler's rule over Germany. Plenty of Nazi plunder made it to America. Decades of battles between museums and alleged heirs claiming rights to a work ensued and could have led to an emotionally charged theft. Nevertheless, this could only be possible if *Nude* turned out to be the kind of art Hitler began expelling from Germany in 1933.

The unregulated art market also attracted the most powerful criminal organizations in the world during the 1960s and 1970s. The Picasso theft came amid a government crackdown on organized crime. In the absence of cash, organized crime stole art to use as collateral to pay for illegal goods and services. Who would squawk at rolled-up art canvases coming through customs in 1973? Apparently, no one, as art passed across borders, a discreet move over a sack of cash, avoiding the watchful eye of the feds.

The theory of stolen art as criminal currency to carry on organized crime schemes wasn't widely held until the end of the 1970s. The Department of Justice and its agencies defined multiple types of various fencing operations that took and sold high-value goods like art.

By the time that information was released to law enforcement, *Nude* had already been missing for four years. The odds of recovery dropped from 20 percent to below 1 percent after five years, and *Nude* was on the spectrum of no return.

MEDIA PRESENCE

Art thefts were usually notable for the haul's size or the heist's audaciousness. Occasionally, its recovery stole the show and made headlines. But cherry-picking unpopular art of famous artists from a collection proved profitable and drew less attention in the news.

The museum could not sustain a media presence long enough for the public to make a visual memory of *Nude*. The small size, generic title, and lack of historic documentation made the painting even more challenging to recover in 1973. Fifty years later, likely no one knows of its sordid past, wherever it went.

Criminal reports of art thefts remained local for quite some time. St. Louis's wave of art thefts started with the stolen Picasso in 1973 and continued until 1978. The last thefts at the museum gained tremendous local publicity compared to the Picasso. But it would be the investigation into the last theft that uncovered a plot to assassinate a historical public figure that garnered national headlines.

In 1979, the FBI initiated the National Stolen Art File (NSAF) to help investigators share information in cases of stolen art. Recently, the FBI launched their internet version for public access. It erroneously listed a Norman Rockwell, stolen two months after the Picasso from a gallery just three miles away. The error sparked a lawsuit in 2007, forcing a famous Hollywood producer to forfeit a painting that was rightfully his to keep. The Picasso stolen from the art museum is still missing from the database.

The 1970s had challenges that made recovering any stolen art difficult. When *Nude* disappeared, it quickly went to the bottom of the caseload of other area crimes. The museum reported the theft two days after it happened, which hurt the investigation. Investigators were at a loss to understand where stolen art disappeared to. By 1979, the crime spree of art thefts in St. Louis ended, as did the case of stolen art that didn't make it into the NSAF.

In recent years, stolen art thought to be gone forever resurfaced after its most recent caretaker died. Perhaps, with the golden anniversary of the stolen Picasso nearing, *Nude* could also reappear under similar circumstances.

But the only way to recover it is to remind people that the theft happened and what the painting looks like. Smartphones, the internet, and social media can make up a lot of lost ground for communications that did not exist in 1973.

The theft's motive could directly impact where it could resurface and if it could be legally recovered to the museum collection. And the only way to understand the motive behind *Nude*'s theft is to dig into the past.

Wherever *Nude* resides today, removing the obscurity of the painting could be the key to her return, and it starts with telling the story of her existence and disappearance.

The Passing of Two Picassos

THE CITY'S ART MUSEUM CURATOR spoke fondly of the Picasso painting as she presented the cyclic nature of art in 1965. Emma Rayburn* described it as a rare Picasso from his early work. Picasso painted *Nude* at the end of his Rose Period in 1906 and shortly before his Cubism phase. His Cubist works featured distorted nudes that barely resembled human figures but were considered Picasso's most valuable works to collect. Near the end of her career as the museum curator, Rayburn again expressed her admiration for the piece and sadness when she discovered it missing from the museum on April 11, 1973.[1]

The outline of a nude woman seated on her knees was slightly contorted. Thick brushstrokes accented her body's shape and high-lighted the contracted muscles. Her chin touched her shoulder as her left arm reached across her body, covering her bare chest. The left hand touched the hair near the right ear, and her right arm was raised above her head. Her left arm, close to her hair, dangled awkwardly, a

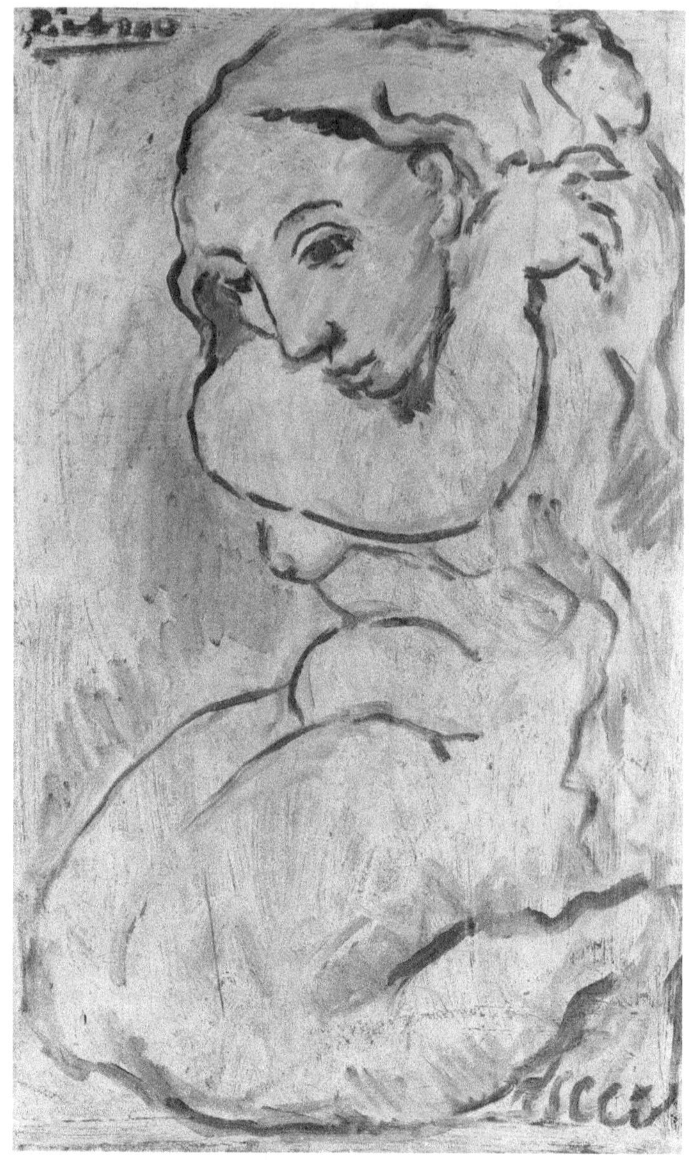

Study for Kneeling Woman Combing Her Hair, *1906*
(*a.k.a.* Kneeling Nude Arranging Her Hair, A Study of Nude or Nude)
By Pablo Picasso, Spanish, 1881-1973 (Oil on wood panel, 8½ × 14¹⁄₁₆ inches.)
© 2023 Estate of Pablo Picasso / Artists Rights Society (ARS), New York.

sign that the artist had not decided how to present the arm that held the hair the woman brushed. The piece was considered a study of the figure but not the artist's final work.

Picasso would create a bronze sculpture of a similar form. The position of the left arm became the distinctive difference between the oil painting and the bronze sculpture. He simply removed the arm from the perspective, resolving the problem. Picasso was in his early twenties when he completed the oil painting and the bronze sculpture.

An interview from the defunct *St. Louis Globe-Democrat* shared Rayburn's recollection of the day the Picasso went missing. She recalled waking to the unpleasant sensation of having the flu—perhaps the onset of a premonition of the bad day the curator was about to have at the museum. Decidedly ill, she left her job earlier than usual, fifteen minutes before five o'clock in the evening. Her office was on the lower level of the east wing. She likely took the closest staircase to reach the main floor, then cut through the Medieval display hall into Galleries 16A and 16 on her way toward Sculpture Hall. As a habit, she often stopped to admire the small Picasso, and this day was no different.[2]

From Sculpture Hall, viewers once stood and looked through the galleries to the end of the museum's wings. Cass Gilbert, the architect, designed each gallery entrance with a grand archway and a deep alcove. Through the years, the alcoves changed to accommodate the growing collection of art, converting the space into mini galleries with faux walls.

In 1973, sculptures were no longer a feature of Sculpture Hall, and it looked only like a lobby to greet visitors. It displayed a welcome desk, a guard's station, and a decorative fountain added in an earlier renovation. The fountain was occasionally filled with loose change from well-wishers.

The museum enclosed the spaces under the tall, arched alcoves with temporary walls to expand exhibits. The unsightly, cubicle-like partitions blocked the view into the museum's wings and created a barrier to the art. Old photos show only a subtle entry into the temporary space from the hall. The alcove exhibits had to be challenging to monitor without standing inside the temporary display room.[3]

Rayburn would have passed through Gallery 16 and entered the enclosed alcove on her way to the lobby exit, passing the painting. Picasso's *Nude* securely hung on a V-shaped temporary wall in this space, at least on most days. As she made her way through the area, Rayburn expected to see *Nude*, but that day, just the two fasteners were on display. No authorization badge was hung in its place, indicating a staff error in the museum's relocation protocol.

The moment after realizing a cherished item had gone missing from its usual spot must have been unsettling. A bit of panic naturally would have set in, triggering a sharp focus to quickly find the Picasso.

The curator hoped the missing badge was an oversight, but her gut told her something was wrong. She confronted the closest guard near the north façade facing Art Hill. He told her that he last saw the painting around four o'clock in the afternoon. Only an hour before, staff showed a group of visitors the artwork on a museum tour.[4]

In 1973, there were only two ways in and out of the museum: the north and south doors. Past renovations blocked the east and west wing exits. A thief had to exit with the painting either at the main doors facing Art Hill or the lower rear doors next to the auditorium lobby. Suspecting that it might still be in the building, Rayburn ordered the guards to secure both exits during the search.[5]

A gallery was only unattended for a few minutes as multiple guards and staff wandered in and out of various rooms. Security protocol typically had one guard at each exit while others roamed the museum galleries. The Picasso room had its own guard, who reported last seeing the painting at four in the afternoon. The thief possibly watched the guard enter and exit the space. Then they may have quickly pried the art from the wall, promptly removed it from the makeshift gallery, then nonchalantly left through the nearest exit.

Rayburn called various departments to check if they had taken the painting and failed to hang the tag. But *Nude* was not securely in their hands. No one authorized it to move.[6] Perhaps someone hid the picture to retrieve it later. Maybe a jokester circulated among the visitors that day, one pulling off an ill-timed April Fools' prank.

An hour had passed since her discovery, and the reality of the situation seemed inevitable: someone quietly robbed the City Art Museum on Art Hill for the first time. The staff wanted to be sure the painting was not on the premises, so they continued searching the following day.

The chief of security at the museum was a former lieutenant in the St. Louis Police Department in the Hampton location, the district that covered Forest Park. He oversaw the immediate investigation and guarded the doors during the search, according to a follow-up article in the *St. Louis-Globe Democrat*.

The following day, museum security guards continued to scour the corners of the entire facility, hoping someone had hidden the painting. They finally notified local authorities of the theft at 10:30 a.m. on Friday the thirteenth.

The art museum's comptroller provided an excuse for the delay. He told the press they wanted to avoid looking silly in the event the painting was still at the museum. The reason was almost laughable until I learned of a similar occurrence in 1979 at New York's Metropolitan Museum of Art (a.k.a. The Met). A visitor easily pried a Greek marble head away from its pedestal and left the museum with it during visiting hours. Security scoured The Met for a day before contacting the New York Police Department.[7]

The NY museum executives, embarrassed by the theft and the potential negative publicity, hesitated to release the information to the public. Two days passed, like the missing Picasso case, before the media got wind of the incident. Similarly, both museums sent out a press release and photos to the media across the country to generate publicity.

The Met took the extra step to locally distribute flyers that described the artwork. The publicity pressured the thief, generating an "anonymous tip" that led the NYPD to a locker at Grand Central Station.[8] Unfortunately, the St. Louis museum did not launch a "lost pet" campaign to create the same local pressure.

If a petty thief stole *Nude*, he would soon get frustrated and abandon the work because it would be too hot to sell locally. Therefore, having it in his possession was a risk. The only way to mitigate that risk was to return it anonymously. "Abandoned art" was commonly followed up with an anonymous tip for recovery. After investigators recovered stolen art, they typically stopped pursuing the thief, so it was advantageous for a thief to make sure the art was returned. Since that did not happen, *Nude* was unlikely abandoned. Whoever took *Nude* intended to keep the painting for themselves or store it until it could be moved to another location and put up for sale.

The late notice robbed the police and FBI of the opportunity to obtain critical clues. Art detectives cite museum thefts as mostly inside jobs, so the delay seemed suspicious. If there was a conspirator inside the museum staff, a forty-two-hour delay would have allowed someone to settle down and organize their thoughts before investigators arrived.

Short of inventing a time machine and returning to the crime scene, it was hard to say whether investigators believed someone pulled off the robbery with help on the inside. The case files no longer exist, and any chance to recover interviews with the staff has also vanished. Any lists of potential suspects were lost in routine file purging. The few reports in the news offered no investigator insights other than general theories about art theft.

In 1973, the FBI report on the theft would have been a local affair. No database existed to share the description of the stolen art across the federal agency offices. The next best thing was to submit it to the Art Dealers Association of America (ADAA) and add it to a list of stolen art, a list that was only circulated to its members.

The choice to steal a Picasso was not surprising. Only three days earlier, Picasso had taken his last breath at the ripe old age of ninety-one while at home in his French château. The theft was an insightful move for a criminal wishing to cash in on the inevitable rise in value for Picasso art. The day after Picasso died, the National Gallery of Art in Washington, DC paid a record amount for a Picasso painting ($1.1 million). The artist's sales over the following years would continue to dwarf that number.

Immediately after his death, there was bound to be an uptick in visits to view his work to pay homage. Anyone understanding the potential increase in value may have gotten a sudden impulse to steal *Nude.* The little oil painting was not the most valuable Picasso displayed at the museum. It was, however, the most convenient in size, easy to remove from a partition wall, and close to the main exit doors in 1973. It was also close to the security station, which resided in Sculpture Hall and just outside the wall where it hung the day it disappeared.

Most thieves target personal collections in homes and businesses, like private galleries. Museums were the least targeted but not immune from robbery. The double-digit rise of art thefts in the United States would have concerned museum leaders, even though the museum was not financially able to add staff or better security systems in the early 1970s.

The FBI believed it was a contract order. They cited stolen art from a museum as something a *fence* could not quickly sell without a buyer already in the wings. A fence was a term for someone who dealt in the purchase and sale of stolen goods. Investigators assumed an economic benefit was the general reason for all art thefts.

I could not find any law enforcement speculating the culprit was a Picasso fanatic wanting a memento of the artist. Passionate thefts were uncommon. But, if one had occurred, the intent would have been to keep the art until death, or at least until the police were hot on their trail. The theft's timing and the length the painting has been gone could indicate the motive for robbery was as rare as the painting.

Exiting the museum during daytime hours was the quietest and least suspicious option to steal from the museum in 1973. The thief only needed a lookout, whether a staff insider or not. Had the thief chosen to steal at night, they would have entered through the glass doors located in either the North or South entrance. A forced entry would immediately alert security staff, who normally guarded the doors after hours.

The years of awkward renovations could have inspired a thief to plan a daytime heist. They need only to pretend to be a regular tourist, one of the hundreds visiting the museum that day. The guards were not in the habit of frisking guests. The extra walls created smaller galleries, possibly hiding the thief from the view of guards, staffers, and other visitors.

Likely, the thief had a lookout as they removed the painting from the wall. The picture was framed, though I found no description that provided what it looked like or its bulkiness. The fastener required the painting to be jiggled from the wall and was not easily removed like a wire hung from a nail. The oil painting was small enough to conceal beneath a spring jacket on that rainy day, safely sneaking it past security.

In 1973, the art museum looked like a concrete vault, a formidable fortress sitting on Art Hill. The building's windowless northeast façade and limited access points created a false sense of security. Despite its rugged appearance, it was old and needed serious repair. A leaky roof, unconditioned space, and lack of natural light were hardly the attractive features Cass Gilbert (the original architect) had in mind. The museum budget lacked enough dollars to bring the staffing size and facility up to par with art museums in other cities.

The daytime theft was bold, but the heist lacked the drama of most movie plots. No one donned tight black clothing and descended a rope from a skylight after museum hours. Though the art museum had plenty of skylights, they leaked and were covered, providing no real risk of access in 1973. No one could backflip, cartwheel, and slither into the gallery space to avoid the web of red beams separating them from the Picasso. The museum had too many walls for acrobats and no sophisticated alarm to monitor the galleries.

Art theft, in most instances, was not the work of highly skilled thieves, as seen in movie heists. Fifty years ago or more, the security flaws in museums made it possible for anyone with a plan and the cojones to steal art. Art thefts were already high across the States when the first robbery occurred at the St. Louis museum. Only Europe had more significant problems. Italy alone was a walking museum, with unsecured churches and antiquated structures hardly capable of protecting the precious works inside.

If thieves could figure out how to get in and out undetected, they could get away with the *Mona Lisa*, and one such thief did just that in 1911. A man working maintenance at the Louvre museum in France slipped into a closet and hid from the sight of museum staff. After the museum closed, he placed the Leonado da Vinci masterpiece under his smock and walked out. The piece went missing for two years. Investigators caught the thief only when he attempted to sell it in Italy. The tale of the theft made the *Mona Lisa* famous worldwide. It also bore the first lesson of art theft: art was uniquely identifiable, and a masterpiece was impossible to sell in the open market.

Thieves can't strip a painting like jewels from a necklace, smelt it like gold, and then sell the loot in disguise. Art has to stay intact to retain its worth. The more it was recognizable or valuable, the harder it was to dispose of to just anyone. The standard assessment for post–World War II art thefts was that an art thief needed a buyer in advance to make quick cash. Lesser works like the stolen Picasso also had a hot period, making an open market sale risky, if not wholly impossible.

INSURANCE FRAUD SCHEMES

Expensive art was an asset, and owners often insured those assets to collect money if they were lost, damaged, or stolen. Insurance companies had customarily paid a portion of the policy's value to cover ransom thefts and payout rewards to anyone who found the art. Some masterpieces were so valuable that the owner could not afford insurance or the insurance company refused coverage.

A broad range of opportunities for insurance fraud has always existed, art being just one avenue to exploit. Many American experts believed insurance fraud motivated about 90 percent of thefts. Thieves stole art and then worked with an accomplice to collect a reward (a finder's fee). The insurance company paid the reward as part of the insurance policy. Some insurance companies went so far as to change their policies to not offer compensation in an attempt to deter a scheme.

Art-knapping, like a kidnapping scheme, occurs when the thief steals art and threatens to harm the art if the owner does not pay a ransom. Thieves used the method more frequently during the 1970s in Europe than in America. It was an easy scheme when money was the endgame. However, quick cash was not always part of the demand. Members of the Irish Republican Army once stole art and held it for ransom in exchange for IRA prisoners.[9]

Though *Nude* was a rare period piece, it was not Picasso's masterpiece. The museum had far more valuable paintings to steal if a ransom was the goal. Not to say it was an impossible motive; the art thief could have prioritized execution over value. At only 8½ × 14 1/16 inches, anyone could easily conceal *Nude* and remove the painting in broad daylight. More than likely, if it were a ransom case, the Picasso would have been returned to the museum, and this book would have a very different angle.

According to the museum director, the market value for *Nude* at the time of the theft was $85,000.[10] That translates to about $560,000 in 2022 currency but excludes any appreciation in value on the open market. The current value would be in the millions assuming the previous growth rates and other factors remained positive.

The museum updated its collection values on record, an important task to reflect changing market values in case of an insurance claim. In the wake of Picasso's death, the museum would likely reevaluate *Nude* closer to $100,000 or more. It was common for a museum to watch similar works sold at auctions shortly after the death of an artist to monitor changes in value.

However, the museum made a critical oversight with *Nude*. The record reflected a value significantly below its actual market value. The director blamed an understaffed team of curators who had the impossible task of maintaining the most current values of their large inventory of insured art. The argument made no difference to the insurance company. They reimbursed the museum just $40,000, a value from 1968, instead of the higher market value for *Nude*.

A reevaluation of all the Picasso art in the museum's possession was bound to rectify the error sooner than later. An insurance company spokesperson told the press the theft's timing was simply a fluke. For the museum, the mistake had to feel like salt rubbed in the wound coming off its first loss on Art Hill.

Pablo Picasso died just seventy-two hours before the theft. The art was bound to skyrocket in the wake of Picasso's death. Even though the museum received less than half of the painting's value, the future value was an incentive worthy of keeping the artwork in its collection and pay a ransom or reward. More than likely, a reward or ransom scheme was never the motivation behind the theft of *Nude*.

The only remaining opportunity for insurance fraud was filing a false claim. The scheme usually occurred with personal collectors, not a public museum. Besides, the insurance claim on the stolen Picasso yielded half of the actual value. If the museum had conjured such a scheme, they would have reviewed the insurance value first to understand the financial gain. In doing so, they would have corrected the policy error beforehand.

Insurance fraud became frequent enough to increase insurance prices for policyholders, leaving some museums to accept less or no coverage for inventoried works. No matter which potential insurance fraud scheme was possible in 1973, none of them were plausible reasons for a thief to steal *Nude*. I safely put the insurance fraud theory to bed.

THE DR. NO THEORY

Another unlikely theory for the theft of *Nude* was a Picasso-obsessed billionaire who hired thieves to steal art. Imagine a cognac-drinking tycoon who retreated to his hidden room each night to secretly admire the stolen work of a master artist. Hollywood perpetuated this idea, but it was one of the least likely scenarios in real life.

Dr. No, the first James Bond book turned into a movie, shaped a commonly held view that wealthy collectors hired thieves to steal art for their personal satisfaction. In the film, Bond passes a Goya painting in Dr. No's lair, a painting stolen in real life when the movie hit theaters in 1962.

The producer meant it as a joke, but it would develop into a widely held belief about who commits art crimes: greedy rich men with an appetite for art. Art investigators call this perception the

Dr. No Theory. Years of investigations into art crime revealed the theory was grossly inaccurate. Most art thieves were far less interesting and sophisticated as those portrayed in the movies. Yet the common belief among the population remains because most of their exposures to art theft were through showbiz.

The extent of the theories involving the greedy rich salivating for art did not stop with *Dr. No.* Another idea arose in the 1960s that art was being stolen and sent behind the Soviet Iron Curtain.[11]

The speculation was the Kremlin looked down upon its citizens with hefty bank accounts. To hide their cash assets, the Soviet wealthy bought stolen art. However, I never came across any notable cases where this actually occurred. In all likelihood, the theory was born out of the Cold War between the US and the USSR.

Lastly, a similar theory existed describing wealthy Brazilians who bought stolen art as an investment to help them skirt excessive taxes in Brazil. The postulation sounds reasonable by today's standards, where wealthy investors purchase art as an asset and stow it away into a tax-free shipping port for similar reasons. However, I also never found any trend from the period of the Picasso theft that supported the theory of tax-evading Brazilians.

Aside from insurance fraud, I decided to eliminate *Dr. No* and related billionaire themes as the motivation behind *Nude's* theft.

LOOKING FOR NEW CLUES

In 1973, there was less than a 20 percent chance of recovery for lesser-known works like *Nude*.[12] Between 1970 and 1974, art crime was on the rise by 15 to 20 percent annually.[13] Once a painting was missing for five years, the chance of a return was less than 1 percent. *Nude* will be officially missing for fifty years in April of 2023.

A local theft motivated by intrinsic value seemed unlikely but not impossible. People have stolen art out of obsession, though it was rare. Maybe someone just wanted a piece of Picasso's legacy in the days after his death. An art patron or student, or even a college prank, could fit the bill of the kind of frenzy to occur in the days following the master artist's passing.

The story of the missing Picasso was a blip in the museum's history, an event most people do not recall. It was almost as if the theft had never happened. Because it disappeared quietly, and the publicity quickly faded away, it was possible the painting had been living in a similar state of existence for all these years.

The little portrait could be sitting in a dusty attic next to a broken chair and a few headless mannequins, reeking of mothballs. Perhaps a child somewhere has yet to realize their grandfather was an art enthusiast of the illegal kind. The treasure could be found if the current owner reads this story and sees the photo of the painting and makes the connection that a piece they inherited illegally once belonged to the art museum since 1934.

The multiple art thefts in St. Louis to follow *Nude's* disappearance reflected an organized event more than a lone opportunist. An art theft ring or organized crime could also be responsible for the missing Picasso. Still, I needed to dig into the city's past to better understand the type of crime operations that existed in 1973.

With a lack of leads in the case of the stolen Picasso, there was not much to go on. Maybe there was something I had overlooked. The curator's interview in 1973 provided information that was the closest to a fresh experience. She shared how she felt, what she saw, and her actions after the discovery. She was one of a few people present and still living the day it happened. An interview could provide new information in the case if she was willing to talk.

When I finally located Rayburn for a quick conversation, her memories of that day were long gone. She remarked that *I knew* more about the case than she did. The response closed the door to new clues from the day of the theft. It may have seemed to her I knew more, but only because the stories of multiple art thefts in St. Louis were fresh in my mind. After speaking with her, I realized I did not even know much about the painting when we talked. Getting to know the victim (the painting) was an excellent place to start.

THE MYSTERIOUS HISTORY OF NUDE

The Saint Louis Art Museum bought Picasso's *Nude* for $900 in early September 1934. The first reference to *Nude* in a catalog came sixty years after Picasso created the painting. One would expect the painting to have been included in the first official catalog of his work: *Pablo Picasso* by Christian Zervos, Vol. 1 (1895 to 1906). Picasso worked directly with Zervos to produce the book he released in 1932, two years before *Nude* came to the museum.

In fact, it would be a 1967 catalog by two other Picasso scholars that first documented the painting. The 1967 Daix and Boudaille catalog sourced *Nude* to the October 1934 bulletin of the City Art Museum of St. Louis. The catalog also listed Theodore Schempp as the collector before it came to the museum. However, news announcements from 1934 never mentioned the art dealer's name or former owner. They merely stated that *Nude* was from a private collector.

A quick Google search revealed Schempp to be an art dealer with a home base in Wisconsin early in his career when *Nude* came to the art museum in St. Louis. His interest in art started when he went to France to study music in 1930. He met artists like Picasso and art dealers like Ambroise Vollard. Schempp dabbled in art and changed his career aspirations from pianist to art dealer. One historical profile of Schempp described his early career days of selling art from the trunk of his car.

Many art dealers, like Schempp, started collecting art as a hobby before turning it into a business. Yet, for a rookie art dealer trying to make a name for himself, it made no sense to downplay the transaction with a notable museum or his ability to access rare Picasso art.

Schempp sold a Matisse to the museum a decade later and admitted to the press that *Nude* was his first sale to the museum.[14] I began to doubt Schempp's identity as the anonymous private collector that owned *Nude* before 1934. I believe the catalog has incorrectly sourced the art dealer's name because the former collector had asked to keep his name private.

I located the museum bulletin, the 1967 catalog's direct source for *Nude's* provenance, fully expecting to see Schempp's name. His name was absent from the newsletter, and the acquisition story garnered no more than two sentences. *Nude's* description was buried inside a short article that lumped multiple September acquisitions together.

The bulletin elaborated on its most significant French acquisition from the period, *La Tante Marie,* by the artist Paul Cézanne. The museum refers to its English title, *Marie Cézanne, the Artist's Sister.*[15] Like the press announcement, it listed a New York Gallery, M. Knoedler and Co., as the dealer to sell it to the museum. It also said the gallery acquired it from Ambroise Vollard.

Vollard was instrumental in the launch of several modern artists, the most famous of which included Cézanne and Picasso. He had a history of buying art directly from artists at lower prices. He held the art for long periods (like an investment) then sold them for a premium price. This included artworks from Picasso's Rose Period (1904–1906).

Vollard's name was already in the bulletin for the sale of *La Tante Marie.* Had he been involved in *Nude's* sale to the museum, the bulletin would have attributed Vollard as the previous collector. I am sure of this because Vollard had a direct connection to *Nude.* He commissioned the bronze sculpture of the same kneeling figure. The authors of the 1967 catalog, the first to reference *Nude,* listed this fact about the painting.

Nude and two sketches of the exact figure were precursors to the bronze sculpture. The sculpture had two French titles: *La Coiffure*

(The Hairstyle) and *Femme se Coiffant* (*Woman Combing Her Hair*). Hence, *Nude's* most recent title, *Study for Kneeling Woman Combing Her Hair*, was logical compared to the other titles.

Like *Nude*, the creation dates of the bronze varied in different reference materials. The bronze sculpture made it into the official Zervos catalog, Volume 1 (1932), with a date of 1905, just as Volume 22 (1970) had dated for *Nude*. Keep in mind that Picasso contributed directly to the Zervos catalog. At least one scholar contends Picasso often confused the dates of the art he created from the Blue and Rose Periods. This would explain why the Zervos catalogs erroneously dated the kneeling figures Picasso sketched, painted, and sculpted to 1905.

Suppose Vollard was the last owner of *Nude*. He was also the previous owner of *La Tante Marie*, and the museum acquired *Nude* and *La Tante Marie* just a week apart. In that case, I am confident the 1934 transaction in the newspaper would not have described Vollard as merely a "private collector."

After reading Schempp's biography, I became even more convinced that Schempp could not have been the private collector described in the old newspaper clippings. As a new art dealer in 1934, he had the incentive to tell the world about the sale of a Picasso to a reputable museum in a large market.

With no evidence to support the theory, I had to move on to the only clue that remained to uncover *Nude's* mysterious past and potentially unlock a new motive for the 1973 art theft. The acquisition year, 1934, was a year in a period that witnessed the most enormous art crime perpetrated on this planet. In 1933, Hitler unleashed a war against modern art, which included works like *Nude*.

Degenerate Art

THE VALUE OF STOLEN ART from the Saint Louis Art Museum between 1973 and 1978 was just a minuscule representation of the financial whole. Worldwide, art thefts climbed at a double-digit rate and were over 34,000 pieces annually by the mid-decade.[1] It took a few years for any notable theft to hit St. Louis museums and galleries. The modern plunder of art consisted of small waves throughout numerous cities and countries, a stark difference between some of the most extraordinary cultural seizures during significant wars.

From dictators to dons, for centuries, dark souls have coveted art for its beauty and value. It has funded war and criminal activity for the past 200 years. In its wake, thousands of artworks remained missing in the gray and black markets.

St. Louis erected its first art museum west of the Mississippi in 1881, near the corner of today's 19th and Locust Streets.[2] Local wealthy businessmen founded the museum. Many purchased or loaned items from their collections to display to the public. Art museums were signs of a sophisticated metropolis and often the cultural center of a prominent city.

The history of art theft started with a similar idea, except power-hungry leaders envisioned their own countries as the cultural center of an entire continent. They plundered art on an impressive scale, forcefully taking it from just about anyone and anywhere.

The first and most notable organized art theft during wartime came at the direction of Napoleon Bonaparte. Napoleon plundered art and brought it back to France, claiming the country as the center of artistic culture. He was the first historically known figure to have an art team commissioned for wartime plunder.[3] He also used stolen art to negotiate treaties with his enemies. The Louvre in Paris benefited from some of the art France retained after the Napoleonic Wars.[4]

Indirectly, St. Louis can thank Napoleon for contributing to the current art museum. Napoleon continued to fund his conquest in part by selling the French-owned Louisiana Territory to the United States in 1803 for a mere $15 million. To celebrate the centennial of the Louisiana Purchase, St. Louis hosted an exposition of the same name. Most people know it as the 1904 World's Fair. To protect the world's art on exhibit at the fair, the Louisiana Purchase Expo Company erected a permanent structure at Forest Park, replacing the first museum on Locust Street.

Shortly after the successful fair, the Louisiana Purchase Expo Company gifted a statue of a famous Frenchman riding his horse into battle. The statue sits on top of Art Hill, centered in front of the north façade of the Saint Louis Art Museum. Thankfully, it was not Napoleon Bonaparte, because it would be really awkward having one of the world's greatest art pillagers guarding the city's art museum.

Instead, the man on the horse was the only king to be crowned a saint— Louis the IX. The city, named after holy French royalty, first settled under the short-lived rule of the Spanish. Like most cities, it became a melting pot of immigrants. About 50 percent of the city's population in 1906 was of German descent. German artists and sponsors were responsible for funding most of the city's monuments, including the man on the horse who symbolically protects the art museum.

The museum's early acquisitions imitated St. Louis's European forefathers, who settled in St. Louis and built the city into a major metropolis at the turn of the twentieth century. Modern works of German, French, and Spanish artists began to fill the museum's collection in the early 1930s. German artists like Beckmann, Ernst, and Kirchner; French artists like Matisse, Degas, Rodin, and Cézanne; and the Spaniard Picasso were on display throughout the east wing of the Saint Louis Art Museum. The timing of some acquisitions came at the lowest point in the history of humankind when Hitler rose to power in Germany.

The Nazis began to take the works of the artists mentioned above from museums, galleries, and personal collections. This was also when *Nude* first came into the possession of the museum in St. Louis. The history of Hitler's so-called degenerate art became the backbone of the modern-day art plunder, essentially leading to other thefts like *Nude*'s.

Nazi plunder began in 1933, immediately after Hitler took power as the country's leader. Hitler ordered his chieftains to take art from museums, galleries, and private collections in his own country. The Nazi regime forced Jewish citizens to hand over their artworks through violence and intimidation. They gathered the non-Aryan citizens, sent them off to concentration camps, and stripped them of their assets; businesses, homes, furniture, books, jewelry, and art became the state's property under Hitler's new decree.

The Socialist Party burdened German Jewish citizens with an enormous "flight" tax, making it difficult for them to leave Germany and seek refuge elsewhere. Some sold their art at meager prices to escape Nazi Germany. Those that went to France, Poland,

Switzerland, Belgium, or the Netherlands were only buying time. Those countries would eventually fall under Nazi control. The first order of business was to strip Jewish citizens of their rights, seize their assets, and deport most of them to Nazi death camps or labor concentration camps.

Degenerate art was the term Hitler gave to modern works he despised. He believed artists suffered from a "degenerate" mind, a characteristic not worthy of his "pure" Aryan race. By comparison, Napoleon was an amateur pillager of European art. Hitler stripped private galleries and museums, starting with those in Germany in 1933, then repeated the act in every country he seized. By the end of WWII in 1945, Hitler and his troops amassed over 650,000 stolen paintings, sculptures, prints, and more.[5] The battle over art and ownership rights began after the war and continues today.

For twelve years, the Nazis stole art and sold modern pieces to collectors and museums in the United States. Once the war ended, the critical effort of reuniting art with its owner began, but it was not an easy effort. Museums that acquired art between 1933 and 1945 had to deal with the reality the art they had purchased (or had been donated) might not be a legitimate transaction.

The acquisition of *Nude* in 1934 and its revolving name added to the mystery of its quiet disappearance in 1973. Did the Nazis strip *Nude* from a German gallery, museum, or private collector before the museum purchased it? If so, could it be the motive behind the theft in 1973?

I began looking for evidence of Nazi-confiscated art in the art museum collection as a place to start. Like all of Picasso's art, *Nude* would have qualified as degenerate art and been confiscated as such. The museum acquired *Nude* in early September 1934, narrowing the opportunity of it being looted to between January 1933 and August 1934. This was when Nazis began removing art from Germany. If it were looted art, it had to come from a location within the country's borders.

THE PROVENANCE PROJECT AND RESTITUTION

Art transactions during Hitler's rule, 1933 to 1945, became a red flag for those looking to recover art and return it to the rightful owner. Also on the list were dealers and galleries known to have dealt with confiscated art. The period overlaps with Europe's Great Depression (1929–1939), which can complicate matters of whether the art was sold under duress of the Nazis or just economic pressures. The immediate postwar era required the return of confiscated art to its original owners, or rightful heirs, though not all museums took it seriously, and some were not cooperative at all.

The paintings confiscated under Hitler and sold to American art dealers, collectors, and institutions were considered modern art, a style that *Nude* fit. The return of art seized in Germany was complicated because Nazis stripped pieces from *German* museums, galleries, and private collectors, and each had different implications for return of the art after the war. Art pieces taken from German museums and sold in the international market were deemed legitimate transactions after WWII, so private collectors and institutions in America were allowed to keep the art.

However, Nazis used intimidation, violence, and other tactics to force private collectors to turn over their art and, sometimes, their galleries. Art procured by these means was considered theft and ordered to be returned to the owner. In many cases, those art collectors were killed as part of Hitler's extermination plan. The heir became the person seeking restitution after the war. Proving restitution in a case was a difficult task.

The most challenging cases of art taken in Germany might have been connected to Jewish art dealers. A dealer who sold art to a German institution that was eventually stripped of the art was legal. If they sold it for financial support, it was *possibly* legal. If they were forced to sell it under Nazi-imposed duress, it was illegal.

The most onerous burden of proof fell upon the shoulders of an heir seeking restitution. They had to provide evidence of their relationship with the victim. Furthermore, they had to prove the victim was the last legal owner and that the art was taken under duress. At times, it created a battle of wills between heirs and museums, those with restitution rights versus those with good-faith purchaser rights.

Museums bought art through reputable dealers, not always knowing the previous owner. Sometimes wealthy art patrons gifted great artworks to the museum. In either case, the art could have roots in theft without their knowledge. Museums spent money promoting, securing, and maintaining art in their collections for years before learning their history. Restitution claims against the art led some museums to quietly sell the art to other institutions or store it away until forgotten.

Legal battles for art were expensive, lengthy, and sometimes never resolved. The frustration on either side of the table could lead to the heir or institution to take matters into their own hands. At least, it was a working theory that could explain *Nude's* quiet arrival and disappearance at the museum.

In 1998, the American Association of Museums (AAM) agreed to publicly identify all pieces acquired between 1933 and 1945. It was an effort to be more transparent for searchers looking for art taken during WWII. The step was long overdue, and the pressure for museums to publicize the provenance of their pieces from this period had come on multiple occasions since the war.

To comply, museums had the task of hiring professionals to track down art transactions, diving into old history to trace their movements. To uncover twelve years' worth of acquisitions in a market lacking record-keeping was time-consuming, I imagine, and quite expensive.

The Saint Louis Art Museum identified nearly 300 pieces in its collection that met the requirements of AAM. The researchers traced the museum acquisitions from the period to legitimate transactions between the art dealer and its previous owner.

Because the museum lost *Nude* to thieves long before the effort to establish provenance, the museum had no reason to commit to researching its history. The transaction date in 1934 narrowed the possibilities of whether *Nude* had also come to the museum as lifted art.

I began using the museum's data to research art from the "red-flag" period. I looked for names of art dealers, galleries, and donors that might cross-reference with those associated with cases of restitution involving art acquired in Germany.

FROM GERMANY TO AMERICA

The Nazis confiscated about 17,000 pieces from German museums, separating modern art from the rest of the haul. The art Hitler preferred was hidden away so that Hitler could someday establish a German museum of so-called acceptable art in Linz, Austria, his hometown. The degenerate art would make its way to America in three ways: auctions, sales to art dealers in New York, or immigration.

To remove what he deemed degenerate art from Germany, Hitler commissioned a team of four German art dealers to dispose of the modern art to be stripped from Germany. The committee stored artworks until they were bound for sale on the international art market.

The Nazis burned about 4,000 modern pieces as acts of loyalty to the new Nazi regime and their own degenerate belief system. The destruction may have motivated art enthusiasts to rescue confiscated art through Nazi-backed international auctions. Public sales of modern art began in 1937, two years before the war began. A few wealthy St. Louis businessmen purchased art sold directly through German-backed art auctions or reputable art dealers.

The Grand National Hotel in Lucerne, Switzerland, hosted the most notable auction of confiscated artwork in June of 1939. It featured modern works from Picasso, Paul Gauguin, and Vincent Van Gogh. It drew collectors, art dealers, and museum curators worldwide.

The work of artist Henri Matisse did not meet the criteria for acceptance under the Nazi regime. His *Bathers with a Turtle* (1908) would never make it in the collection slated for the Führermuseum in Linz.

The grandson of newspaper magnate Joseph Pulitzer Sr. (of Pulitzer Prize fame) purchased *Bathers with a Turtle* at the auction. He donated it to the Saint Louis Art Museum in 1964.[6] The Folkwang Museum in Hagen, Germany, displayed the art before being stripped of its modern works. The German museum's curator purchased it directly from Matisse.

Private collectors and art dealers from the United States purchased works of renowned artists at the Lucerne auction. Many buyers, like Pulitzer, believed they were saving art destined for destruction. It was also an opportunity to get art at reduced prices.

Though Hitler hated modern art, members of his staff confiscated some of the pieces for themselves and sold stolen art to other Nazi officers. During the process of immigration, looted art made its way to America.

A prime example of the difficulty of restitution was the case involving the painting *Das Soldatenbad* (1915), translated *The Soldier's Bath*, by German artist Ernst Ludwig Kirchner. It landed in the hands of Kurt Feldhäusser, a Nazi soldier.[7] The piece came from a stock of confiscated art at the Ferdinand Möller Gallery in Berlin.[8]

After Feldhäusser died in a bombing raid in Nuremberg in 1945, his collection was passed to his mother. She brought the group to North America and consigned this piece to the Weyhe Gallery in New York in 1949. Another prominent St. Louisan, Morton D. May, purchased *Das Soldatenbad* from the gallery in 1952, a post-WWII period of increasing demand for modern art.

May, a philanthropist, was the CEO of The May Company, having its headquarters in St. Louis since 1905. (The May Company became part of Macy's in 2005.) May had one of the largest collections of German Expressionist art and donated them to numerous institutes. In 1956, he gave *Das Soldatenbad* to the Museum of Modern Art (MoMA) in New York City. The museum displayed the painting under the title *Artillerymen*.

MoMA then moved it to the Solomon R. Guggenheim Foundation in 1988. Around eighty years after the Kirchner piece had been taken, the painting finally returned to the heirs of the original owner, Alfred Flechtheim, in 2018. The family sold it at Sotheby's for nearly $22 million.

Aside from *Das Soldatenbad*, Morton May also purchased Kirchner's *View from the Window* (1914)[9] and *Circus Rider* (1914) from the Weyhe Gallery. Both came to New York via Feldhäusser's mother. The Nazis took the former piece from the Hamburg Art Gallery and the latter from Municipal Art Museum, Mönchengladbach, in 1937. May willed the two works to the Saint Louis Art Museum in 1983.

May also donated *Village on the Sea* (1913), a work of German artist Karl Schmidt-Rottluf.[10] The Nazis confiscated it from the National Gallery in Berlin. The former Prussian Crown Prince Palace was repurposed as a modern art museum in 1919. It held the works of Schmidt-Rottluf and his peers until July 7, 1937, when the Nazis stripped the pieces from the walls. The war brought total destruction to the gallery only after its contents were emptied and sent to auction. *Village on the Sea* made it to the Buchholz Gallery in New York in 1939 and was sold to May in 1950.

The Pulitzer and May donations to the Saint Louis Art Museum came to the States under Hitler's decree in Germany. The art was sold at auctions or stateside galleries three or more years after *Nude* came to the museum. These sales transactions remained legal after the war and did not qualify for restitution. Knowing that the museum had pieces directly connected to the "red-flag" period, I continued to dig into the possibility of *Nude* somehow being confiscated in Germany.

CURT VALENTIN, ART DEALER

Before Hitler came to power, Curt Valentin, a German Jew, was an associate dealer in a Jewish-owned gallery in Berlin. Karl Buchholz was a second German art dealer tasked with disposing of degenerate art from Germany. In 1934, Valentin went to work for the Buchholz gallery in Hamburg, Germany.

Art scholars have varied opinions about Valentin. Some describe him as a professional art dealer with a tremendous positive impact on the art world. Others contend he was the most significant force behind the sale of modern art looted by the Nazis, shipped to America, then sold for profits.

Likely to save his life, and perhaps the works of modern art, Valentin made a deal with the Nazis. He immigrated to the United States to sell degenerate art in the safety of New York. Buchholz paid for Valentin's passage to America. Valentin brought some art and opened a modern art gallery in New York City in 1937 named Buchholz Gallery.

The timing of the move also aligned with another important date in the modern art plunder. In one significant effort, Hitler's minister of propaganda, Joseph Goebbels, sought to remove all modern works from German galleries and museums. In just a few days, Nazis seized about 17,000 pieces in July 1937. The highly regarded works of Picasso, Vincent Van Gogh, and Henri Matisse became part of the art purge in Germany. The Nazis did not favor native sons like artists Max Beckmann and Ernst Ludwig Kirchner.

Valentin was one of several dealers to represent Beckmann during the years just before Hitler's takeover. Like Picasso, Beckmann was a highly regarded painter when Hitler rose to power. He began teaching at the Academy of Fine Art in Frankfurt in 1925, but the Nazis ousted him in 1933. He exiled himself from Germany. Two years after the war ended, Beckmann took a job at the St. Louis

School of Fine Arts at Washington University at the invitation of the Saint Louis Art Museum's director.

Over 650 pieces of stolen art made up the *Degenerate Art* exhibit, which toured Germany and Austria from 1937 to 1941.[11] Works that did not make it into the show went to auction and were sold to foreign markets. The auction funded the Nazi war machine unleashed on Europe in 1939.

Max Beckmann's *Christ and the Sinner* (1917), on display at the Saint Louis Art Museum, had the unfortunate history of being an exhibit piece. Beckmann originally sold the work to the Mannheim Art Gallery of Germany, but the Nazis confiscated the painting on July 8, 1937. Like all other confiscated work, the Nazi thieves assigned an inventory number, 15936, a sad reminder of how they also serialized and tattooed Jewish citizens upon entering concentration camps. The painting landed in the first room of the *Degenerate Art* exhibition in Munich.[12]

Valentin acquired the Beckmann painting in 1938 for the Buchholz Gallery in New York. He sold art to numerous museums and collectors in the States during WWII. In 1944, authorities seized multiple artworks from the Buchholz Gallery in New York under the Trading with the Enemy Act.[13]

Around 1951–52, the Buchholz Gallery name changed to the Curt Valentin Gallery just a couple of years before Valentin died.[14] In 1955, the City Art Museum of St. Louis paid tribute to Valentin with a special exhibit featuring works acquired through the art dealer. The director praised Valentin's taste, knowledge, and integrity in the January/February bulletin documenting the event and the featured art. The show blended works from both the museum and private collections on loan.[15]

As expected, there was no mention of Valentin's controversial arrival in America. Nor had it revealed his gallery was under the previous ownership of Buchholz, a Nazi art dealer in charge of confiscating and disposing of "degenerate art" taken in Germany. It would be an inappropriate message to pay tribute to Valentin, who bequeathed *Christ and the Sinner* to the museum in 1955.

Plenty of evidence supported art confiscated from Germany came to the city's art museum via donors and art dealers. However, the art

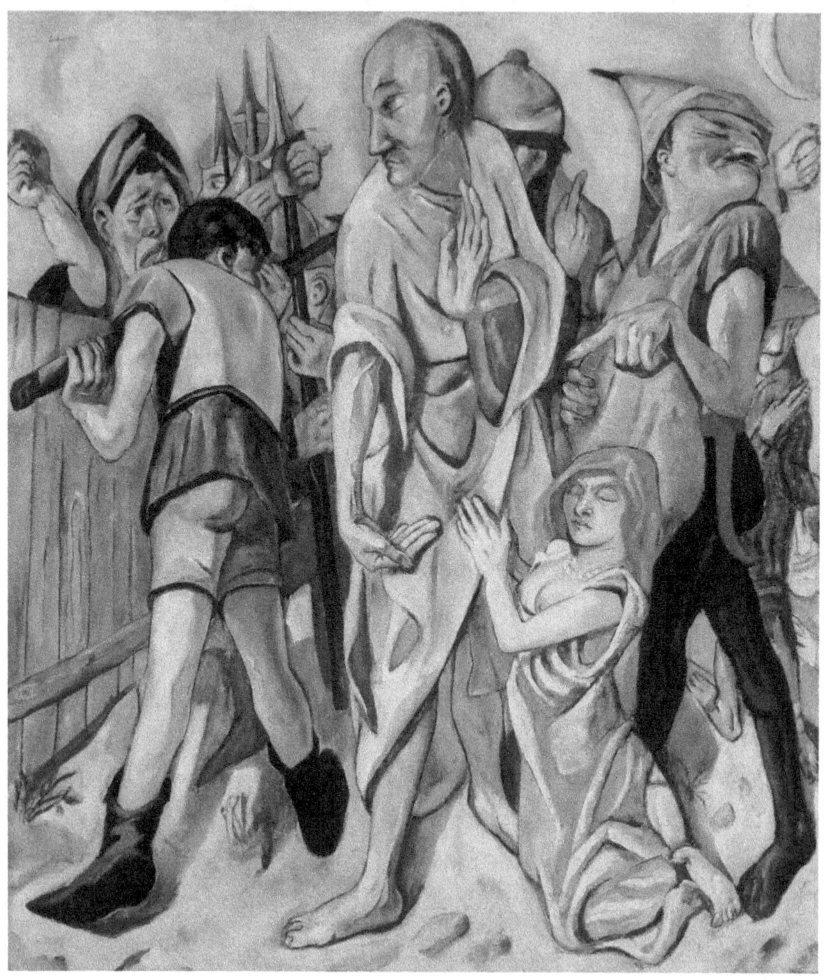

Christ and the Sinner *(1917) By Max Beckmann, German, 1884–1950*
Oil on canvas; 58¾ × 49⅞ inches;
Part of Hitler's Degenerate Art exhibition
Saint Louis Art Museum, Bequest of Curt Valentin 185:1955.

came from Germany's museums, either from international auctions or immigration, all legal acquisitions. Additionally, the transactions occurred years after the museum purchased *Nude*.

If *Nude* came from Germany, it had to come from another channel to get into Schempp's hands by 1934. After digging into the art museum's provenance project and cross-referencing art dealers and donors with looted Nazi art, one name seemed to fit the profile as potentially the previous owner of *Nude*. A considerable force behind the modern art movement in Germany, he fled the country in 1933: Alfred Flechtheim.

Valentin worked for Galerie Flechtheim of Berlin before 1934 for several years. Flechtheim was the original owner of Kirchner's painting *Das Soldatenbad*. He exhibited Beckmann's work on many occasions, along with the other German artists listed in the provenance project. Lastly, Flechtheim dealt exclusively with modern art, mainly by twentieth-century French artists, but not excluding Picasso, who lived and painted in France.

ALFRED FLECHTHEIM, ART DEALER

Before becoming an art dealer, Flechtheim was an avid collector of modern works. He learned about the trade as he spent time in Paris, where he befriended German artists. He returned to Paris in 1907 and met Pablo Picasso and his newest art dealer, German-born Daniel-Henry Kahnweiler.[16]

Soon after, Flechtheim built his collection of Picasso paintings and other works of modern artists to fulfill his goal of becoming a dealer. When the first world war derailed his plans, he closed his Düsseldorf gallery. He sold his collection of 250 works at a Berlin auction, including the collection of Picassos. The war sent him to Belgium as a German soldier, but he was too old for the front battles, so he worked in administration.

After the war ended, he finally reopened his gallery in Düsseldorf. Eventually, he expanded to new locations, including Berlin, Frankfurt, and Cologne, Germany. He was thriving under the Weimar Republic, the last democratic government in Germany before WWII.[17]

Flechtheim was at the center of the art scene in Germany. He represented modern artists, making deals with galleries and other dealers in Paris, London, and New York. His success began to wane around 1925. He had to tighten his belt on the heels of the stock market crash in 1929 and the ongoing depression in Europe. By 1932, he was forced to close two of his galleries. His Düsseldorf and Berlin locations remained open.[18] Nevertheless, the worst was yet to come for the dealer.

Flechtheim had dark eyes, olive skin, and a prominent nose. He was unapologetic for being Jewish. Nor was he ashamed of his love for modern art. Two significant strikes against him in the eyes of the National Socialist German Workers' Party. The party that rose to power in Germany in the early 1930s blamed Jewish citizens for Germany's economic troubles.

Flechtheim bought, sold, and exhibited works of Beckmann, Kirchner, Picasso, and more.[19] As a pioneer behind the modern art movement, several German artists put the dealer's likeness on canvas as a sign of respect. German artist Otto Dix painted Flechtheim transacting an art sale.[20]

The painting showed the dealer in a brown suit with tan flecks as he stood behind a desk with a painting at his side in his left hand. It showed only the painting's corner, but enough to recognize it as modern art. He gently lays loose papers upon the desk with his right hand, signaling a transaction for the art. A painting within the painting hung on the wall, another modern piece wrapped in a classical frame, honoring Flechtheim for his contribution to the modern art movement and the support of those artists.

Hitler believed the modern art movement was a symbol of society's degradation. This included works of Impressionism,

Post-Impressionism, German Expressionism, Abstract Art, and Cubism, among other modern genres he deeply despised.

Flechtheim's success as a modern art dealer and pioneer ended with the Nazi Party and the appointment of Hitler as Chancellor of Germany. On multiple occasions, Flechtheim became the subject of Nazi propaganda. The Socialist Party newspapers wrote malicious articles about the art dealer for being Jewish and a staunch supporter of modern art.

Between December 1932 and January 1933, *Illustrierter Beobachter,* a newspaper of the Nazi Party, featured Flechtheim's face on the cover twice. The December edition alone featured his face in two photo montages meant to represent him as the typical Jew, plotting a conspiracy of global Jewish domination: an utterly unhinged view of the Nazi Party.

Hitler became chancellor less than thirty days after the January article. In February, Hitler's new decree restricted personal freedom, including freedom of expression. The state had control over private property. Anyone infringing on the order faced prison or death.

By March, the Nazi party held the majority seats and was ready to wield their power for destruction. Hitler soon gained control through legislation and killed democracy in Germany. With the dictatorship in place, the whole reign of terror against a race of people and their art began immediately.

In the same month, unruly mobs attacked Flechtheim's Düsseldorf gallery during an exhibit. One protestor threw a bomb into it. Fortunately, it did not hurt anyone, but it rattled Flechtheim, perhaps for the first time. He was no longer safe in Germany.

The Nazis targeted Flechtheim for financial ruin immediately after Hitler's takeover. Unable to conduct business, he faced bankruptcy. In April of 1933, another propaganda rag story happily reported his economic destruction, calling for his extermination. He fled Germany that May, leaving his wife behind. He did not have enough money to pay the "flight tax" required for his wife to go with him to Paris, France.

The bank creditor in Germany seized his gallery assets in Düsseldorf and confiscated his remaining collection. Much of it sold through the international art market, some retained in the ranks of Nazi officers. He managed to get a few pieces out of the country, hoping to start a new gallery.

After failing in France, Flechtheim headed to London and began working for Picasso's art dealer, Kahnweiler, at Galerie Simon. He traveled between there and Paris for work and organized art shows, including Picasso exhibitions, up until 1936. He also managed to slip in and out of Nazi Germany to occasionally see his wife. After an unfortunate accident in London, he landed in a nursing home where he would die in 1937.

Flechtheim became the earliest target of Nazi public harassment, leading to his art being scattered worldwide. Even though he was dead, the Nazi hate for Flechtheim continued. Flechtheim's face appeared on posters and catalogs promoting the tour of Hitler's degenerate art, reinforcing the criticism of the previous republic. The traveling show of degenerate art started in 1937 and ended in 1941.

Flechtheim had connections in America. He was a friend of Alfred Barr, the director of MoMA in New York City. He wrote Barr in 1935 and told him he lost his money and pictures when the Nazis took over his Düsseldorf gallery. He even tried to sell a sculpture to Barr. Barr's response to Flechtheim's plight was not empathy. He believed he could get the piece for less.[21]

Then there was Valentin, Flechtheim's former senior gallery assistant. Valentin represented Buchholz Gallery and Barr to acquire degenerate art auctioned in Lucerne, Switzerland, some of which would include art from Flechtheim's gallery. Some scholars speculated Valentin was a vital force in selling art to American collectors, whether private or public, once he came to New York. Still, Valentin didn't likely have anything to do with the sale of *Nude* to the museum. He was still in Germany in 1934.

If *Nude* had been stripped under Hitler's decree and made its way to the States via immigration, it likely would have been near the war's end, not the beginning. The chances of the painting slipping into the United States in 1934 as Nazi-looted art out of Germany seem minuscule.

Suppose the art had been in Flechtheim's possession before 1934. In that case, it couldn't have come to America the way most modern artworks arrived during Hitler's reign. The plight of Flechtheim from Germany to Paris, France, in 1933 was the last potential window of opportunity for *Nude* to have made its way to Schempp, the art dealer credited with the sale to the museum in September 1934. Schempp was in Paris starting in 1930, but I was unable to determine for how long or if he ever crossed paths with Flechtheim.

Kahnweiler and Flechtheim owned works together over the years, splitting the sales' profits. The Parisian art dealer also sent Flechtheim artwork for his galleries in Germany to be sold on commission. He also remained the most compelling reason for the painting to have made it into Flechtheim's hands. The first opportunity might have been as early as 1907, when he met Kahnweiler. *Nude* was painted shortly before that time, and Kahnweiler was newly representing Picasso's artwork. If Flechtheim possessed it in the early 1900s, it would have been sold in the Berlin auction before he left to serve Germany in WWI.

The second potential opportunity was if *Nude* had been in Flechtheim's gallery on loan from Kahnweiler. Sources I found stated Flechtheim fled with just three pieces to France to restart his business in 1933. Yet *Nude* didn't seem to be a choice of painting to rebuild a career in France, as Flechtheim had access to more valuable art.

The research satisfied my curiosity of whether the missing Picasso could have been Nazi loot. *Nude* did not come from Germany, nor was it eligible for restitution. I eliminated it as the motive to steal or hide the missing Picasso from the art museum. Even if Flechtheim sold *Nude* to Schempp, there was no reason to protect his name as the collector in 1934. Flechtheim was still alive and working for Kahnweiler in Paris.

After an exhaustive search, I can only imagine what the museum must have gone through trying to track down the transactions of hundreds of works for the provenance project. The project started long after the theft of *Nude* from the museum, so there was no point in it being included in the project. The lack of documentation and the inconsistency of information made finding out the provenance of *Nude* harder than I imagined.

The Saint Louis Art Museum purchased several pieces in the late summer of 1934 to build the French Impressionist and Post-Impressionist collections. This included *Nude* and several other works, acquiring them just a day apart. The museum purchased paintings from Jean-Louis Forain, André Derain, Mary Cassatt, Edgar Degas, Georges Rouault, and Charles Dufresne for just over $2,000 combined. I hoped at least one of these purchases might provide clues. Since the pieces were acquired a day before the Picasso, perhaps the art museum documented the history of those pieces in the provenance project. Their history could contain new information relative to *Nude's* acquisition, but unfortunately, the museum sold all the pieces long before the research began.

I contacted the museum multiple times, hoping they could find an old file in their archives. I was looking for any information to validate Schempp as the collector or find a name for the collector he represented. Though I felt comfortable eliminating *Nude* as Nazi-pilfered art, I considered the name of the private collector unresolved.

Multiple museum renovations have occurred since 1973, and the painting was *deaccessioned,* a term to describe the official removal of a piece from a museum's collection. I had to consider the possibility they purged their records. Perhaps I would never learn the name of the mysterious collector or discover his reasons for choosing a rookie dealer like Schempp to sell a Picasso under anonymity.

3

CHAPTER

Swindled Art

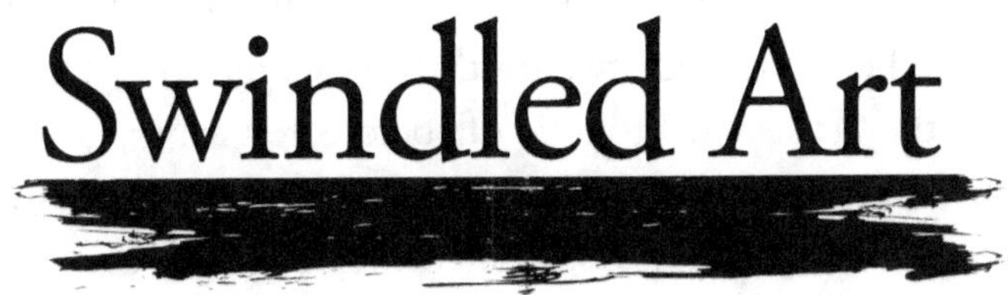

NUDE ARRIVED TO THE CITY ART MUSEUM IN 1934, but it brought a history with it not yet fully explained. It was not degenerate art, stripped from a German museum, gallery, or private collector and sold to the museum. But finally, I would have an answer. After museum staff returned from the pandemic shutdown, a staff member sent me the name of the private collector. I then learned five critical facts from the painting's provenance:

1. The missing Picasso from the art museum has several names, but the official name was *Etude pour Femme Agenouillée se Coiffant,* or *Study for Kneeling Woman Combing Her Hair.*

2. Picasso painted *Nude* during his Rose Period, art created between 1904 and 1906. According to Picasso, he painted *Nude* in 1905, though scholars believe the correct date to be 1906.

3. In 1934, Wisconsin art dealer Theodore Schempp sold the painting to the museum on behalf of an unnamed collector for $900.

4. In 1967, the first catalog published a picture of the painting and listed the City Art Museum of St. Louis as the owner. It also wrongly identified Theodore Schempp as the previous collector.
5. In 2022, the museum fulfilled my request and located a small file leftover from *Nude*. A 1965 memo named German artist Dietz Edzard as the private collector.

To understand more about the history of *Nude*, I turned to the painting's subject, Fernande Olivier, a model and mistress to Picasso. Fortunately, she wrote a book, *Loving Picasso: The Private Journal of Fernande Olivier,* describing their life together, including the years of the Rose Period.

Olivier had posed for multiple artists when she met Picasso in 1904, when they were both twenty-three years old. She had a brief affair with the artist and broke it off before returning to his arms in the late summer of 1905. When 1906 arrived, she professed her growing love for Picasso but also related their struggles as a couple.[1]

Picasso was still relatively unknown. Picasso refused to let Olivier model for most other artists, so they both lived off whatever income he earned from selling his art, which was very little. In 1906, Olivier described in her memoirs their financial state as poor.

In the spring of 1906, the art dealer Ambroise Vollard visited Picasso's studio and purchased twenty paintings for 2,000 francs. Olivier wrote in her journal that they were rich. This was a typical reaction of a young adult with no money, and they spent it without reservation.

The income prompted Picasso and Olivier to visit Barcelona to see his family and friends in May 1906. Picasso vowed not to return to Barcelona as a failure, so with money and a fiancée, he headed home for the summer. After a short visit, the couple headed to another small town, Gósol, for a working vacation.

During Picasso's time in Gósol, he transitioned his subject of young males in his art to female subjects. Specifically, he created numerous pieces depicting Olivier, beginning in Gósol.[2] This was likely the main reason for scholars attributing *Nude* to 1906 and not 1905.

Picasso and Olivier, still in love, returned to their everyday life: financially broke and struggling. Before the year ended, Picasso painted Olivier in the kneeling nude position, using a black and white palette of oils on a sheet of wood about the size of a legal-size paper. *Nude* represented one of the last paintings created during his Rose Period.

In 1907, Picasso and artist Georges Braque developed Cubism. The new style moved away from a singular form and replaced it with a series of geometric shapes and interlocking planes. Soon after, Picasso's art began to shift. Olivier's image took an angular shape in his work as a precursor to his next phase.

At first, critics hated the movement. The scathing publicity in newspapers probably did a lot for turning Picasso into a household name worldwide. The relationship between model and artist also began declining and ended in 1911.

Picasso was ready to put that part of his life in his past. Soon after, his financial luck began to change. Enough people were over the shock of the modern movement, and Picasso was well on his way to becoming a world-famous artist. Picasso's economic status when he painted *Nude* differed significantly from when he died. The artist left behind quite an estate, including multiple chalets, a castle, and thousands of artworks never seen. The amount of his total estate was estimated at $250 million in 1973, a wealth he began to accumulate after his time with Olivier ended.

Even when the art museum acquired *Nude* in 1934, Picasso was already a wealthy and renowned artist. On the other hand, Schempp, the art dealer who sold the painting to the museum, was a rookie art dealer. Maybe the museum never mentioned Schempp's name publicly because it didn't carry the weight of a Vollard.

Schempp studied art in France in the 1930s. He was good friends with Georges Braque. He knew Picasso and the art dealer Ambroise Vollard, but they were not the source of the painting. Instead, it came from a German artist, Dietz Edzard.

Edzard studied art with Max Beckmann in 1911, and German Expressionism influenced Edzard's art. After recovering from the first war, he moved to Bavaria, where he developed his artistry. He even exhibited at Flechtheim's gallery in Berlin a year before moving to France in 1928. Starting in the 1930s, he showed his art in New York, London, and Paris. At thirty-five, Edzard began having international success as an artist, but the world knew Picasso, then forty-eight, as an artistic genius and a master of his craft.

France was undoubtedly the location for gifted artists of all kinds: musicians, writers, painters, and sculptors. Schempp was a pianist turned artist, then an art dealer. Edzard and Schempp most likely met in Paris. To understand why Edzard would want his name held from public disclosure when he sold to the museum had to do with one more criminal scandal.

Picasso's mother, Dona Maria, took care of a good portion of Picasso's early collection, which included 681 drawings, 200 paintings, and seventeen sketchbooks in her Barcelona home.[3] That changed in April 1930 when a Spaniard named Miquel Calvet showed up at the home of Dona Maria and acquired some of Picasso's early work. Soon after, the artist was embroiled in a legal battle that the French press dubbed *L'Affaire Picasso*. It started in 1930 and lasted until 1938.

Calvet acquired over 401 pieces of works from Picasso's childhood home. Most were drawings, but Calvet left with at least ten paintings in the con. Calvet sold the lot to Madame Zak of Galerie Zak, but she purchased them on behalf of Edzard.[4]

Edzard bought the entire Picasso collection obtained by Calvet for 200,000 francs (approximately $7,849). He paid Zak up to

20,000 francs as a commission. To cover his expenses, Edzard permitted Galerie Zak to sell seventeen drawings and three paintings for 220,000 francs. This would have left him with a significant Picasso collection at no cost.[5]

Galerie Zak sold one of those paintings, *Barcelona at Night,* to an art dealer named Bernheim. The art dealer then asked Picasso to sign the painting. When he asked, he told Picasso he got the picture from Galerie Zak, which had acquired multiple pieces of his work.

Picasso headed to Galerie Zak. When he entered, he immediately recognized the items from his "juvenile" period that only could have come from his mother's home. He saw sketches of his parents and art created before he wanted to be an artist. Picasso was upset. Unlike the other art he signed, he had a sentimental attachment to what he saw in Zak's gallery.[6]

He told Madame Zak he would return and sign the art. Instead, Picasso returned with local authorities to seize it.[7]

On May 9, 1930, Picasso filed a complaint against the Spaniard Calvet, claiming he acquired the art under false pretenses. Picasso reported to authorities that Calvet and an American man showed up at his mother's home in Barcelona that April. They asked to borrow the collection for a study on the early works of Picasso and to reproduce a book. His mother thought she was doing the right thing and released the 401 pieces to Calvet. In return, Calvet paid a small fee for her assistance.

Picasso was wrong about the American man. It was a French art dealer and critic he had met in Paris, Joan Merlí. (Merlí would eventually write about the early works of Picasso.) Picasso would later testify he learned of the sale *after* signing some of the pieces for another dealer, who claimed to have acquired them in France through Galerie Zak. Jadwiga Zak, the widow of a Polish artist, started and owned the gallery Picasso named in the complaint.

Calvet's side of the story was he went to the Barcelona home with Merlí, looking to buy some Picasso art. Picasso's mother offered him an extensive collection of drawings and a few paintings for 1,500 pesetas. This was about 5,000 francs or the equivalent exchange rate of about $196 in 1930.

Many of the drawings, Calvet declared, were in lousy shape. Most of the pieces still needed Picasso's signature, and Calvet argued the works were worth almost nothing without it, a statement meant to justify the low price he offered to Picasso's mother for the collection.[8]

A month had passed between Calvet's acquisition and Picasso's formal complaint. During that time, Picasso signed multiple pieces of art. The artist told the press he often signed pieces from his youth left behind at galleries. When asked to sign specific paintings (acquired through Calvet), Picasso said he did not attach any particular importance to them. "I did not even remember where I might have left them."[9]

Learning this, I believed how easily Picasso could have signed a painting like *Nude* if it came from the art Calvet swindled from Dona Marie in Barcelona. *Nude* was one of the multiple pieces in his study of the kneeling figure, but not the final piece, and relatively insignificant.

Picasso also had a good reason to let *Nude* go into someone else's hands. In 1930, Olivier published a series of memoirs, *Picasso and His Friends,* in a weekly Belgian publication, *Le Soir*. Picasso vehemently opposed the idea and only payment to Olivier persuaded her to stop, at least until 1933.

Picasso never questioned the source of the painting when he signed the art. Instead, someone told him the art came from Galerie Zak. The dealers receiving the works testified they had either arranged or already met with Picasso for signatures. The initial investigation lasted for almost two years.

The Zervos catalog (Vol 1.) was photographed and produced between 1930 and 1932 for Picasso's artwork expanding from 1895 to 1906. The 401 pieces tied to *L'Affaire Picasso* were unavailable for the book because they were under court control (361) or missing (forty). *Nude* was also excluded from the book. Perhaps *Nude* was part of the works Calvet acquired from Dona Marie in April 1930 then sold to Edzard.

At the end of 1932, the judge discharged all parties, but Picasso quickly appealed. The appeal forced Calvet before a Spanish criminal court in 1932, where the judge rendered him guilty and sentenced him to two years, a sentence Calvet appealed.

When Picasso asserted his claim for the works held by the court, he found Edzard also claimed the art as his property. As a fellow French-based artist, Edzard should have known better to question Calvet and the legitimacy of the bargain acquisition. The only route for a Picasso collection of this size before 1930 was through one of Picasso's reputable art dealers. Edzard planned to restore some of the art acquired from Calvet. This included cutting some of the sheets featuring multiple studies into separate, smaller units.[10]

When authorities seized the art, they took 191 pieces from Zak's gallery, then 150 more drawings from Edzard's apartment.[11] Edzard sold twenty works to recover his investment, but the court ordered most buyers to return the art.

Together, 361 works of art were under the court's possession until the ownership issue could be resolved. It also meant forty pieces had made their way into the market, unaccounted for in the 401 pieces Calvet obtained in Barcelona.

Madam Zak sued Picasso in 1936 for libel, demanding damages for 200,000 francs, the amount paid to Calvet for the pieces. Whether the courts settled the dispute was unknown. By 1941, the Nazis invaded France. They liquidated her museum and sent Madame Zak and her son to Auschwitz, where they died in 1944.[12]

Picasso initiated proceedings against Edzard in 1936 for the title of the works seized six years earlier. A 1936 American press news clip summarized the court action, stating the court awarded the art pieces to Picasso. The court officials said Edzard should have questioned the low price.[13]

Edzard appealed, but the court upheld the results in 1938. The same year, Calvet began serving his sentence. He served only as a prisoner of Spain, a country he remained free to roam as long as he never left during his two-year sentence.

It would seem that the mysterious provenance of *Nude* might have had a criminal history before it even came to the St. Louis museum. The timing of *L'Affaire Picasso* aligned with the museum's acquisition of *Nude*, and Edzard chose to remain anonymous in 1934 amid litigation with Picasso.

Nude could have been part of the disputed collection from Picasso's boyhood home in Barcelona. Or coincidentally, Edzard could have acquired the piece before the 1930 scandal and decided to part ways with it quietly through Schempp during his legal battle with Picasso.

When Picasso filed the complaint against Calvet, he described the confiscated art as being from 1903 or earlier (his juvenile period), but not without the possibility of error. Picasso came across the juvenile work when he first arrived at Galerie Zak, and this motivated Picasso to file the complaint. It doesn't mean all of the art Calvet acquired in Barcelona was from the same period.

Finding a second source regarding *L'Affaire Picasso,* I discovered the court returned the Barcelona collection to Picasso in 1938. Spain was experiencing a civil war, and the Nazis were on the brink of starting a war in Europe. This kept Zervos and Picasso from publishing the catalog of the art held by the court until 1954.

Zervos catalog Vol.6. (1954) was the first supplement to Vol. 1.[14] For a second time, *Nude* did not make the Zervos catalog that covered Picasso's work up to 1906. The painting had already been in the museum's hands for twenty years.

Among the sketches in the Vol. 6 catalog were two similar poses to *Nude*. The catalog listed the art as *Mine de plomb* (translated graphite) and attributed the art to Picasso's time in Gósol, 1906. If the sketches came from *L'Affaire Picasso*, it proved *Nude* could have too.

Maybe Picasso painted *Nude* in Barcelona or Gósol and left it behind with his mother. It was also reasonable to consider Picasso moved some of his early art featuring Olivier into his mother's home. Olivier represented a period of struggle, and maybe he wanted to leave those memories in the past. Barcelona seemed like the perfect place to store a painting of an ex-mistress—far away from the current mistress.

The case of Picasso and Calvet started four years before the museum acquired *Nude* and ended four years after they acquired it. This put the transaction right in the middle of the eight years of litigation over the art Calvet conned directly from Picasso's mother in Barcelona.

If *Nude* had been a part of the Calvet acquisition, it would explain Edzard's desire for anonymity and why he chose a rookie dealer like Schempp to sell the art to the museum. Schempp, located in Wisconsin, was far away from the art scene in New York.

The sale to the museum happened when Edzard needed to distance his name from Picasso and quietly keep the source of the transaction from the press. The press ran articles and updates on Picasso's legal battle in France, Spain, Belgium, Britain, Germany, Poland, and the United States. Edzard's career was on an upward path, his art featured in prominent exhibits, including tours in the States.

Even if Edzard owned *Nude* before *L'Affaire Picasso,* the publicity of a sale of a Picasso in the middle of the lawsuit could have made him look suspicious. I can't say with one hundred percent confidence that Calvet acquired *Nude* from Picasso's mother and sold it to Edzard in 1930.

Without a doubt, I can say that the ownership battle for hundreds of works from Picasso's childhood home in Barcelona brewed between Picasso and Edzard when the painting came to the City Art Museum. The former owner was intentionally labeled an unnamed private collector, a move that kept Edzard's name out of the press as the previous owner of the Picasso.

Edzard died in 1963, four years before any catalog carried a picture of *Nude*. Two years later, the museum curator, Rayburn, who discovered Picasso's *Nude* missing in 1973, left behind the note that named Edzard as the private collector. Her memo, dated 1965, was the same year she gave a lecture about the museum's bargain acquisitions from the early 1930s. The talk, featured in a St. Louis newspaper, mentioned *Nude* as a purchase from the period.[15] Given that the memo was dated years after the transaction, I assumed Rayburn reached out to Schempp, who provided the name of his late client in 1965.

When I set out to solve the mysterious disappearance of *Nude*, I never imagined the mystery I would uncover would be a scandal from 1930 that may have brought the piece to the museum. Though the battle between Picasso and Edzard was not the motive for the 1973 theft, it likely contributed to the painting's obscure history and delayed documentation in the Zervos reference books. As the golden anniversary of the art theft approaches, maybe the story of *Chasing Picasso* can bring *Study for Kneeling Woman Combing Her Hair* home to the Saint Louis Art Museum.

Understanding the painting's provenance gave *Nude* a personality. It was no longer a black and white oil figure on canvas. Knowing the painting was created in Picasso's early career when he was poor made it more likable. The kneeling figure was no longer a faceless model. Instead, she was someone the artist once loved, adored, and then resented. The potential of it being involved in a very public criminal affair made the stolen Picasso a more complex piece of art than first realized. All of which could add value to the painting.

The Enigma of Art Value

IT WAS REASONABLE TO QUESTION WHY ART, just as gold or diamonds, was highly valued by humans yet attributed little to basic human needs. Unlike other products, each piece of art was identifiably unique. Artists created art for the public to view and appreciate, but it had no functional purpose nor did it demand regulatory oversight. Artists, dealers, and buyers were free to conduct transactions through an art dealer, gallery, private collector, or auction in the open market.

Soon after WWII, art enthusiasts worldwide began buying modern works of art in the open market. The boom created a shortage of French Impressionist works, contributing to rising art prices. The short supply and high demand were not the only culprit that led to high prices. Auction houses, traditionally known for the unglamorous sale of just about anything—livestock, tobacco, antiques, estates, and worse, humans—revised the art auction then drove wealthy collectors to moments of absurdity. Art prices soared to new heights, leaving some art unobtainable to museums.

The art market was highly unusual compared to the pricing structures I had experienced in other markets. Each product was unique, so putting a price tag on a piece required guidelines based on various traits. This included material, age, popularity, and history. The final distinction, and the most volatile, was the buyer's value on the art. Essentially, the value of art was worth whatever someone was willing to pay for it.

TRAITS THAT TRANSLATE TO VALUE

Art collectors prefer authentic pieces from popular artists. The discovery of an authentic doodle by Picasso on a restaurant napkin, no matter how small or ugly, would still carry more monetary value than my child's giraffe depiction from her elementary jungle-animal period. *Giraffe with No Legs* might not be worth a sale, but it was priceless to this parent. Many parents would agree that some of the best visuals on display came under the command of an elementary school teacher. An art expert would refute this opinion with evidence of the applied technique of a seasoned artist versus that of a creative child yet to master her fine motor skills.

One event that increased a painting's value was the artist's death, though a famous artist didn't have to be dead to see his work valued. Picasso was a very wealthy man before he died, leaving a considerable estate behind. Cézanne and Van Gogh, however, were not.

Death typically increases the value of the art because the artist can no longer produce new pieces. Someone stole *Nude* only three days after Picasso died, which could explain the painting's rising worth as a motive for the theft. Months after *Nude* disappeared from the art museum, another of Picasso's Rose Period paintings sold for $720,000 at a Sotheby's auction, setting a record, albeit a temporary one.

The artwork's antiquity contributed to higher prices if well-maintained, especially when the artist was renowned. *Nude* was over 115 years old as of this writing. If still in good condition, it could carry a value much higher than $673,000, a price solely adjusted for inflation for the last stated value of $150,000 in 1978. Recent auction prices for Picasso's art from the same period indicate *Nude* could garner much more if it still exists.

A painting with color, especially red, carries a higher value than other colors. For example, the stolen *Nude* was a black and white oil painting on wood. Picasso painted *Nude* during his Rose Period, where most of his works contained a red hue, except this one. *Nude* may garner more money in an auction for its rarity of missing red in a Rose Period or perhaps less for lacking it.[1]

Picasso created two similar sketches to *Nude* as part of his study on the kneeling figure of a woman with her hands arranging her hair. The oil painting and sketches were the precursors of the figure he sculpted in bronze. The artist's choice of media influenced the asking price, with oil paintings carrying a higher market value than sketches.

Vollard commissioned multiple bronze sculptures of the figure from the original cast before it was destroyed (a common practice to limit the reproduction quantity). The oldest sculpture produced would be considered the most valuable, assuming comparable conditions. If someone created a new cast from the original bronze, the new reproductions would carry less value as a second-generation piece.[2]

The oil painting of the kneeling figure was one of a kind, so the value could be worth more than the statue. Still, *Nude* was a study of the pose, and the bronze sculpture was its final form. It was hard to assess which piece would carry a higher price. Multiple bronze sculptures were produced, but only one oil painting. The default answer would be *Nude*, as oil paintings were generally sold for more in the open market and were unique creations.

A painting of a woman sold for more than a portrait of a man, typically. However, the rule didn't apply if it was self-portrait of a well-known male artist. The artist's most popular style at the time of sale was worth more than their other work styles. Picasso's Cubism pieces sold for more in 1973 than his art from the Rose Period (like *Nude*).[3] Like artists, the popularity of the art genre would ebb and flow, impacting market prices.

Those who set retail prices also consider the history of the art, referred to as the provenance. The provenance determined the authenticity of past ownership, tracing the legitimate transfer from owner to owner. The upper class commissioned art for royal palaces, worship halls, courtyards, and prominent architectural structures. Art that had survived centuries of war and pillaging could draw an obscene amount of money.[4]

As art passed from one owner to another, it often lacked the proper documentation, so the older the piece, the sketchier the provenance. The lack of documentation created real problems for collectors and curators. A gap in provenance could be harmless, but it could also signal art that had been stolen, forged, or misidentified. As with *Nude,* the origin of ownership was lacking, and the catalog references of the year Picasso painted *Nude* were inconsistent. Still, there was other art with more significant gaps and questionable history.

The history of ownership played a role in value. A piece from an art museum carried more weight than one from a gallery unless the private collector was well-known. If I owned a Picasso and sold it to Oprah Winfrey, my ownership would not add value to the piece. If she sold it to anyone else, the value would automatically increase. The previous owner, if renowned, added value to the artwork and could add brand value to the artist's other works, like a product endorsement.[5]

THE ART DEALER

Van Gogh sold just a few paintings and drawings during his lifetime. He mostly lived in poverty then committed suicide at age thirty-seven. Cézanne's work only became popular near the end of his life. On the other hand, Picasso benefited from the income his art demanded during his lifetime, starting as a young artist. They all have one thing in common…Ambroise Vollard.

The twentieth-century art dealer was a critical promotor of Impressionist and Post-Impressionist artists to art collectors. Van Gogh died three years before Vollard opened his gallery, but Vollard would help popularize his work. Vollard also purchased a lot of work from the aging Cézanne, breathing new life into his career.

Picasso had multiple dealers, some he favored more than others. Among the favorable were Vollard, Flechtheim, Kahnweiler, and Paul Rosenberg.[6] Though Vollard was not Picasso's agent of record, he launched his career during the time he painted *Nude*.

Historically, art dealers have come in many forms. Some were helpful to the movement of modern art, assisting with the careers of artists, and others exploited their work for monetary gain. In contrast, artists struggled to feed themselves. Then there was the shady art dealer who dealt stolen art to the open market to unsuspecting buyers or to the black and gray markets to suspicious characters.

The art dealer can contribute to an artist's popularity and genre, both critical features of appraising the market value at any given time.[7] The art dealer was the primary channel for popular art sold to collectors and museums in 1934 until auction houses gained their share of the market in the late 1950s.

However, I began to understand why investigators believed unethical art dealers were behind most art thefts. Numerous dealers were cited for cooperating with the Nazis to sell stolen art. Calvet, who swindled Picasso's mother in 1930, claimed to be an art dealer. Vollard died in a suspicious car accident in 1937, and the executor of his estate happened to be an art dealer/Corsican mafioso.

I wondered who came first: the legitimate art dealer who turned to the dark side and sold stolen art or the legitimate criminal who became an art aficionado and disguised his racket as a legitimate business.

THE ART CRITIC

Mel Brooks' *History of the World, Part I* opened with a skit of a Neanderthal man drawing art on the cave wall. In his baritone voice, the actor Orson Welles announces the "birth of the artist." Seconds later, another caveman appears on top of a rocky ledge, staring down at the image. He studied the art with a discerning focus. Welles continues in his methodical voice-over: "With the artist's birth came the art critic." Then to the artist's dismay, the caveman art critic proceeds to urinate on the cave art. It was an image seared into my mind as the role of the art critic, the judge of what was good and bad art.

Sometimes art critics were the nemeses of aspiring artists and, other times, their greatest endorsers. The market has never considered art criticism an attribute to determine the price, even though professional comments about an artist or the art certainly affected popularity. The critic's opinion has always influenced the art deemed worthy of exhibit and sale. The art critic could kill the career of living artists then bring it back to life when the artist was six feet under.

Early on, critics blasted Picasso and his Cubist art. In 1911, *The New York Times* published an article on the "eccentric" movement exhibiting at the Paris Fall Salon. One critic said of Picasso's art, "His canvasses fairly reek with insolence of youth: they outrage nature, tradition, decency. They are abominable."[8] Other critics described the Cubists as disease-minded and degenerate, a decade before Hitler made it a category of art confiscated by the Nazis. Eventually, Cubism art became acceptable and highly valuable.

Critics did not always appreciate the artists of their time, like those in the Impressionist era. It took wise art dealers like Vollard and Flechtheim to promote modern artists and open-minded art critics to accept and appreciate the modern art movement as an evolution.

Hitler was a close-minded, self-appointed art critic of all modern art, hell-bent on ridding Europe of its existence. Art patrons supported modern artists with their pocketbooks in the post–WWII era, in a silent "up yours, Hitler" moment, inadvertently creating a shortage of art. Thus, high demand and low supply increased the value of popular art, and a significant impact on the rise in art values began after the war.

THE UNPREDICTABILITY OF ART VALUES

As an investment, art had cycles, and owning a piece simply for financial gain came with risks. Negligence in maintaining a work of art could damage and lessen its value. A hot artist would become cold, dropping the investment value of his art. Aside from a pure forgery, finding out scholars have downgraded the artist's work to a master's student became a real risk, especially as technology evolved to reexamine art's authenticity.

A 1950s catalog from the Saint Louis Art Museum proudly attributed a full-color oil painting of *A Portrait of a Young Man* (1662) to Rembrandt, the Dutch master. The artist painted the portrait a few years before his death (1669). The museum enthusiastically acquired *A Portrait of a Young Man* in 1950 for $130,000. Owning an original Rembrandt painting can garner national notoriety for any museum. Going to the museum required visiting the authentic Rembrandt, at least up until around 1999.[9]

Thieves, forgers, and painting analysts have frequently targeted Rembrandt's work. A team of Rembrandt experts examined hundreds of the artist's works to determine authenticity. They discovered many works previously attributed to Rembrandt were actually from his workshop and partially created by his hand or not at all.

Near the end of the twentieth century, the experts reattributed Rembrandt's *A Portrait of a Young Man* to an anonymous student

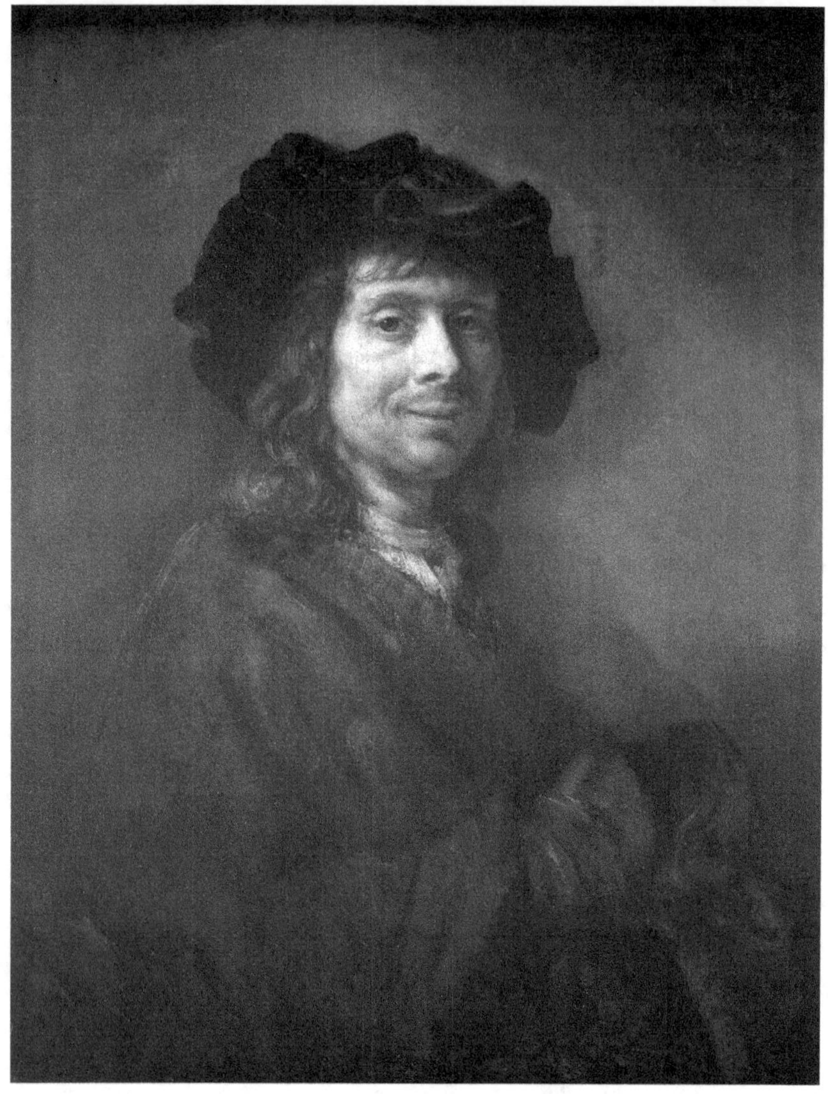

Portrait of a Young Man (perhaps an artist) *(1661–1662),*
workshop of Rembrandt van Rijn, Dutch, 1606–1669, oil on canvas;
35⅜ × 27⅞ inches; Saint Louis Art Museum,
Purchase and funds given anonymously 90:1950.
Reattributed to a workshop piece, circa 1999.

in Rembrandt's workshop. Having a "Rembrandt" in the collection for fifty years, only for it to be reattributed to something less than the master's work, had to be a complete disappointment. The only positive news might have been a less expensive insurance policy on the painting.

Similarly, a Pennsylvania museum had its Rembrandt, *Portrait of a Young Woman,* downgraded during the 1970s. Layers of restoration hid the evidence of Rembrandt's actual work. Through the recent use of X-rays, infrared, and electron microscopy, a new analysis helped reattribute the original work as a Rembrandt.[10] With the discovery came hope for other pieces to be reexamined; perhaps *A Portrait of a Young Man* will rise again to its former glory.

Modern technology could spot forgeries and workshop pieces or unveil hidden art of famous artists, but it was not a perfect science. The master artist guided the workshop and sometimes physically contributed to the pupil's work. Occasionally, the master produced a version in the class, and the pupil contributed to the work of the master. Then there were the students who successfully mimicked the master's technique and fooled the experts. The lack of documentation and repeated restoration created further confusion as time passed. It made investing in a centuries-old painting risky.

Art of the old masters, like Rembrandt and Leonardo da Vinci, seemed at the most risk of misidentification with student work. By comparison, Picasso's art was relatively young. Still, over 1,100 pieces of Picasso's art were lost to thieves over the decades, and the risk of misidentification exists. Picasso influenced an entire generation of modern artists and art forgers. It's possible artists attempting to mimic the master might one day have their work confused with Picasso's authentic art. For all these reasons, the Christian Zervos catalogs of Picasso's are critical to art historians. Eventually, missing art might just come back around for validation.

THE VALUE OF A MASTER'S ART

Art pricing was made of tangible attributes, while art value was whatever someone was willing to pay for it. But some collectors were willing to pay unbelievable amounts to have a Leonardo, Rembrandt, or Picasso. Most of us couldn't imagine spending that amount on art or having a bank account balance that afforded such a hobby. The trickle-down effect of what collectors would pay ultimately impacted other art produced by the same master. *Nude's* value in 1973 was likely a drop in the bucket compared to what a collector might be willing to pay for it today.

In 1934, the museum purchased that little *Nude* for just $900. According to the inflation calculator, it would have been the equivalent of $2,982 in 1973 and almost $20,000 in 2022. However, demand for a Picasso makes it worth far more than the adjustment for inflation. I am not an art expert and have no comparable Picasso to hand over to an expert for evaluation. I learned that the missing Picasso might be worth millions using past figures and an annual compound interest calculator.

The insurance policy listed the painting's market value at $40,000, a figure last updated likely in the late 1960s. In 1973, the museum director estimated the market value rose to $85,000 *before* Picasso's death. In 1978, a museum source updated *Nude's* market value at $150,000 (about $673,000 in 2022 currency). To keep it simple, I calculated the compound annual growth rate (CAGR) between the two figures for September 1934 and January 1978, resulting in a 12.52 percent CAGR. If it maintained the growth rate, going from its last known figure in 1978 to 2023, the painting's value could be close to $30.3 million. Seems unrealistic, right?

Thinking this estimate might be way off, I decided to look at another Picasso Rose Period piece bought at auction in 2004, *Garçon à la pipe* (*Boy with a Pipe*). Picasso painted this in 1905, a year before he painted *Nude. Garçon à la pipe* was a much larger oil painting, close to 3 × 3 feet, painted on canvas, and had more color. It sold for $30,000 in 1950. By then, *Nude* (using 12.52 percent CAGR) would have had an estimated value near $6,000. I used the two figures to demonstrate the monetary gap between two different Picasso paintings from his Rose Period in 1950.

In 2004, *Garçon à la pipe* went to auction at Sotheby's. The initial speculation was the art could go for $70 million, equating to about a 14.36 percent CAGR from 1950. Logic, of course, goes out the window when considering the golden rule of art: It was worth whatever someone was willing to pay for it. It sold for $93 million ($104.1 million, with commission). That was about 14.96 percent CAGR since the previous owner purchased it in 1950. The estimated value for *Nude* might not be as farfetched as first thought.

Garçon à la pipe set a record in 2004 for the most expensive painting sold at auction. However, auction houses often reset the art sales record since 1958, so it was a short-lived feat. The reigning champion as of 2022 was *Salvator Mundi.* The provenance of the painting was a story ripe with lessons about the art market and far more entertaining than explaining the enigma of the art market through a traditional history lesson.

Salvator Mundi, Latin for *Savior of the World,* was the perfect title for a lost Leonardo painting. It went missing over a century ago, died when someone attributed it to a workshop student, then rose again in reattribution to Leonardo. It was the most extraordinary story of unpredictability in the art market.

A New Orleans couple purchased *Salvator Mundi* from a 1958 Sotheby auction in London for the estate sale of Sir Francis Cook for just $120. It was an oil painting accredited as "After Leonardo da Vinci."[11]

A past scholar, I assumed, attributed the piece to a student of Leonardo, either from the time of Cook's ownership or perhaps earlier. The workshop artists painted under direct instruction, sometimes even contributing to the master's work. Researchers attributed between twenty and thirty paintings of Salvator Mundi to Leonardo's workshops. The couple who purchased it passed it on to an heir. The heir put it up for auction then probably fainted after learning it was a Leonardo.

In 2005, a perceptive New York art dealer spotted the oil painting in a minor New Orleans auction catalog. He compared the photo of the oil painting to a 1700s etching of the same title, *Salvator Mundi*. The etching's artist cited Leonardo's painting, *Salvator Mundi,* as the source for his own design. The Leonardo painting was rumored to be missing for over one hundred years. The composition of the etching and the painting featured in the catalog were very similar designs, prompting the art dealer to buy the painting for $1,175.[12]

When he finally laid eyes on the artwork, he could see it was old, and it needed the hand of a restoration artist to skillfully remove some of the layers. Once in her hands, the restoration artist began to uncover layers of the painting. She was sure the figure's lips matched Leonardo's work.[13] This prompted further investigation into the painting's authenticity. Not many Leonardo paintings have survived, and a rediscovered one would be easily worth millions.

After restoration, five Leonardo da Vinci scholars reviewed the painting in person to determine if it could be authentic. One expert decided it was a Leonardo. Another proclaimed it was from a workshop piece led by Leonardo. The three remaining experts remained unsure. With only one expert supporting the claim, a prominent London museum featured *Salvator Mundi* in a Leonardo exhibition. It headlined as the lost Leonardo painting.

The painting, purchased for $120 in 1958 and $1,175 in 2005, gained authenticity as a Leonardo through the opinion of one expert and a prestigious gallery's Leonardo exhibit. Soon after, the owners shopped it around at $180 million, but the controversial attribution kept buyers at bay. With no takers, they listed the painting for sale in a Sotheby's catalog for $130 million.

The lost Leonardo was a fantastic tale of volatility in value. Reattribution to Leonardo, the backing of a prominent museum, and a storied return after one hundred years influenced the value of the painting.

Many other valuable features were present too: it was a rare oil painting with red parts created at the hand of a master artist. Jesus Christ, the prominent figure, added intrinsic value (i.e., an emotional connection for the viewer). However, $130 million was just a list price, and the painting was only worth whatever the next owner offered.

The history of ownership was incomplete and further called its authenticity into question. Any art museum director in their right mind would not touch an expensive piece without knowing if it was authentic. The heartbreak of having a painting de-authenticated was hard enough. Explaining a possible bonehead buy to the board, donors, and taxpayers that fund such purchases would be career suicide.

Another development in the postwar years was that art became an investment to diversify a sizable financial portfolio. A Russian businessman came across *Salvator Mundi* in the Sotheby's catalog and wanted the art as an investment. He turned to his trusted French art dealer who had purchased other artistic assets in his collection.

The Russian investor acquired art under a shell company to keep his name anonymous. Furthermore, he stored art securely at a free port, where no one would see the art again unless he chose to display or sell it.

A shell company is only a business on paper, has no employees, and holds passive investments, such as art. A "free" port is a tax-free designated zone created to stimulate the economy. Wealthy art patrons store art in a free port to avoid paying taxes on art sales.

Free ports treat art as if it is in transit, avoiding taxes and duties usually associated with imports. Governments consider free ports an essential part of international business. However, they are also aware of their seedier uses: fraud, tax evasion, and money laundering.

Art is an international currency because it holds the same value in every country. The owner could use art as collateral and exchange it for items like narcotics and illegal arms in more nefarious situations. Criminals use shell companies in schemes to launder money, so the combination of the two (shell companies and free ports) also draws the interest of international law enforcement agencies.

Like free ports, shell companies are legal business options used in the art market. Someone who invested in art and holds it in a free port isn't necessarily a crook. Like most wealthy people, they understand the tax loopholes or hire someone who does.

The Russian turned to his French art dealer to acquire *Salvator Mundi* in 2013. The role of the art dealer had been the oldest and most common sales channel for art.[14] The French man did not do the actual negotiations with the painting's New York owners. Instead, he used a skilled poker player to read the room, which effectively negotiated the final price of *Salvator Mundi*. When discussions ended, the art dealer acquired the painting for $83 million—a smart move that was perfectly legit and, indeed, would have made the investor quite happy if that was the endgame.

However, the art dealer didn't sell the painting to his client for $83 million. Instead, he communicated a series of fake negotiations via text messaging to his Russian client. The dealer told the investor he was able to get the catalog price down to *just* $127 million. The client accepted the offer, then paid a commission of 2 percent off the negotiated price as a fee, bringing his total investment to $129.5 million.

Aside from the art dealer's commission off the "faux" price, he made another $44 million when he flipped the art in the final sale to his client.

Paying a commission off a negotiated price was a common practice. However, whatever that commission structure was, it would likely not yield a larger payout than his scheme to buy low and sell high to the client. The dealer received a commission on a price he set based on negotiations that never took place. It was an act that crossed the line from sales tactic to intentional deception, an artful move by a shady dealer.

Art attracted both wealthy collectors and the kind of people who preferred to take advantage of their wealth. In the ordinary course of business, Sotheby's did not give out figures for private purchases. This policy essentially aided the French art dealer in buying low and selling high to his Russian client. It took a curious reporter wanting to know what happened to that lost Leonardo. He learned a private collector bought *Salvator Mundi* and managed to get the price range, which he then published in an article.

The art investor was unveiled as a Russian oligarch, a term used to describe a business magnate who had accumulated wealth and power after the Soviet Union disbanded. Imagine his response when he read a story showing a range far below his purchase price for the so-called Leonardo.

The Russian art collector sued the art dealer. His disgust was enough to part ways with *Salvator Mundi*. In 2017, he put the painting up for sale through another channel: a high-profile auction house, Christie's of New York.[15]

Lines of people stood outside Christie's to get a sneak peek at what the press dubbed the male *Mona Lisa*. The promotion of the upcoming auction entailed a video of the painting emotionally moving the spectators who filed in to see it displayed at the New York auction house. A teary-eyed Leonardo DiCaprio appeared among the spectators, linking one famous Leonardo to another.

The emotional hype played on the painting's intrinsic value, creating tremendous publicity for the auction. It subtly reinforced the painting as special—perhaps so special that only an authentic Leonardo could have made people cry.

It worked. People packed the room to see the auction of *Salvator Mundi* and the bidding war between anonymous suitors. The opening bid started at $75 million. It quickly increased in increments of millions, a jump unlikely to have been seen before. When the two final bidders squared off, the last bid was $30 million more than the previous bid, and the auctioneer enthusiastically proclaimed it sold for $400 million. The total price tag was over $450 million with Christie's commission. The sale price shattered all previous auction records for art.

Scholars still disagree on the painting's authenticity. Some believe it was a real Leonardo. On the opposite end of the spectrum, some contend Leonardo never painted any version of *Salvator Mundi*. In between the two extremes are beliefs that it was a workshop piece, which may or may not include paint strokes made by Leonardo's hand.

Salvator Mundi himself might consider the auction behavior to be a blasphemy of artistic creation, though it would still not explain how a painting's value increased 600 percent in eighteen minutes. That enigma required more than one scientific study to unravel what possesses art collectors to lose control at auctions.

Neurologist, avid porcelain collector, and author Dr. Shirley M. Mueller wrote about the auction process in her book *Inside the Head of a Collector*. One fascinating chapter included brain research on motor activity and reward responses during bidding. Functional magnetic resonance imaging (fMRI) was used to scan this part of the brain during a bidding exercise. The results showed a significant increase in brain activity during high bidding. Basically, the fear of losing generated more activity in the reward center (the striatum) and drove a person to bid higher.[16]

This biological research was a subset of another study using behavior economics (a study of monetary behavior using psychology and social science). The research used three groups to compare behavior.

Group one was the control group, with participants bidding in an auction under normal circumstances. Researchers told group two that if they won the auction, they would get fifteen dollars.

They labeled group three the "Loss-Frame" group. They gave them fifteen dollars in advance and said they would forfeit the money if they lost the bid. The results showed that the Loss-Frame group consistently engaged in higher bidding.[17]

Perhaps the fear of losing *Salvator Mundi* contributed to the significant jumps in pricing that occurred in those last eighteen minutes on the auction block. The platform of a highly publicized auction had to heighten the fear of losing. Similarly, Picasso's *Garçon à la pipe* went for $23 million more than anticipated in 2005.

To explain how auction behavior changed from getting a good deal to overpaying, we must travel back to 1958, the same year the misattributed *Salvator Mundi* sold for $120 in a Sotheby's estate auction. Back then, the typical estate auction drew bargain hunters looking for deals on just about anything. Art auctions were fairly routine sales and mostly uneventful and tedious proceedings. In fact, mostly art dealers, not auctions, primarily handled art sales, but that would change in 1958.

Sotheby's entered the auction business in 1744. In 1958, Peter C. Wilson, chairman of Sotheby's, had a brilliant idea to turn the mundane auction into a celebrity, black-tie, Saturday evening affair. Sotheby's deployed closed-circuit televisions to accommodate the overflow of attendees who viewed the event from other rooms. Sotheby's auctioned a Cézanne for more than fivefold the previous record price for a painting sold at auction.

The auction house set and broke the world record for a fine arts sale in one evening and in less than thirty minutes. Seven Impressionists' masterworks were on the auction block that evening. Adding to the ambiance was the ballroom gala, which differed sharply from the traditional auction. Wealthy art patrons rubbed elbows with celebrities, including Kirk Douglas, Anthony Quinn, and Lady Churchill.[18] The atmosphere was charged, and so were the bank accounts of those caught up in the competition of not losing to someone else.

The idea of the auction as a marketable event, where the upper class intermingled with celebrity guests, was an immediate success. The seller and Sotheby's auction house earned large profits under the new auction format. Even artists benefited as their other works increased in both demand and value.

Wilson inadvertently created a perfect sales model, setting a continuum of record sales for over sixty years. The new format was a deadly combination of large wallets and oversized egos under pressure to be the king of the hill when the gavel fell. It drove art values to unbelievable heights.

News of soaring art values translated to potential profits for thieves. They saw unsecured art as an easy, highly profitable score. It spawned the modern-day take that still ravages museums, collectors, and cultural sites. The well-publicized art auction became a significant catalyst for the art epidemic to follow.

Two years after Sotheby's marketing breakthrough, a band of art thieves began ravaging southern France. The event marked a new era in art theft and left a mark on the Saint Louis Art Museum in 1962. Picasso's *Nude* may have been the first piece stolen from the art museum in St. Louis, but it was not the first stolen from its collection. That title belonged to Cézanne's *La Tante Marie* in 1961.

A French Secret on Art Hill

AT THE TOP OF ART HILL IN FOREST PARK and directly in front of the north entrance of the Saint Louis Art Museum, the holy king of France, Louis IX, overlooks the Grand Basin. Sculpted upon his head, the Crown of France rests on his chained armor. His horse was dressed for battle. His royal sword was raised above his head as if to protect the art museum from thieves. But, alas, he couldn't even hold on to his weapon.

Despite his tough-guy stature, the king lost his sword more than three times during the 1970s.[1] It was also a time when parks across the country fell into disrepair. Highways, high rises, and high crime overran many of them. Vandalism of statuaries became the norm. Even Forest Park began hiding its collection of monuments in the maintenance shed for protection against vandals and thieves. The stolen painting from the park's art museum was one of many types of art to disappear during the same period, but its theft was not the first art crime to dip into the collection.

The Apotheosis of St. Louis, its formal title, was originally a plaster statue made for the World's Fair and the creation of Charles Henry Niehaus. It sat where the Missouri History Museum sits today in Forest Park, greeting fair attendees at the main entrance at Lindell Boulevard. The artist designed the original piece to not have a life beyond the exposition. He was paid $4,000 for what was intended to be a temporary statue. The Louisiana Purchase Exposition Company (LPEC) gifted the city a permanent version of the figure on October 4, 1906, but not without controversy.

Niehaus quoted $90,000 ($2.5 million in 2022) for a bronze version, but the exposition company was not interested in paying the high price. They sent the work to the Winslow Brothers Co. of Chicago to cast the bronze *Apotheosis* at more than half the artist's quote.[2]

The artist didn't take kindly to LPEC copying his art without permission, so he initiated a lawsuit and asked for $125,000 in damages. Eventually, he settled for only a $3,000 compensation, and his name was inscribed on the pedestal. This made *The Apotheosis of St. Louis* the first notable local art theft, albeit a copyright infringement.[3]

The first piece of physical art stolen from the collection of the Saint Louis Art Museum happened to occur in the king's country of France, specifically, the region of his queen, Margaret of Provence. Strangely enough, it would be Cézanne's *La Tante Marie*, another 1934 acquisition of French art. The theft uncovered a secret about the painting and exposed a band of criminals set to wreak havoc in the art world.

The day after the museum acquired *La Tante Marie*, the *St. Louis Globe-Democrat* published a photo titled "A $7500 Piece of Art."[4] The headline's tone indicated a hint of sarcasm. It reflected either a distaste for modern art or spending money so soon after the Great Depression. The museum had been on a buying spree in 1934, collecting works of French Impressionists and Post-Impressionists. Modern art had yet to reach a mainstream audience stateside. These became some of the first modern genre artworks in the museum's collection—a wise investment as the values of Impressionist works soared after WWII. Unfortunately, the higher values also attracted thieves to the art market, and most collectors were hardly prepared to defend their valuables.

Modern artists like Picasso considered Cézanne the father of modern art (one of the few facts I retained from two semesters of art history in college). Picasso admired Cézanne greatly and even purchased a castle in 1958, Château of Vauvenargues, near Cézanne's birthplace of Aix-en-Provence. Picasso could see the mountains Cézanne preserved in his paintings from the château. The château became Picasso's final resting place in 1973, though he lived and died in Mougins, France.

The Pavillon Vendome of Aix-en-Provence invited the Saint Louis Art Museum, among other museums and private collectors, to participate in a Cézanne exhibition in 1961. The St. Louis museum loaned *La Tante Marie* for the display. On the one hand, the museum probably felt honored to have the painting present at the celebration in the artist's hometown. On the other hand, the risk of damage or theft was a genuine concern when they loaned the painting to the Vendome.

In eighteen months between 1960 and 1961, thieves stole around $7 million (1961) in paintings in southern France. It started in April of 1960 when they took twenty pictures from the Riviera Hotel Colombe D'Or Inn and Golden Dove Restaurant.[5]

A young Picasso and other struggling artists exchanged paintings for food, room, and board early in their careers at the hotel. Authorities estimated thieves hauled between $400,000 and $600,000 from the hotel in 1960, a value in today's dollars of $3.8 million and $7.6 million, respectively. The following February, nineteen stolen paintings were found in Marseille's railroad terminal luggage room. Thieves may have left them behind when they discovered they were too hot to sell, and the owner had no insurance to pay a ransom.

Criminals stole other paintings and collectibles from a gallery in Cannes, France. In Nice, they took twenty-four pieces from a collector's villa, but police recovered them shortly afterward. The thieves abandoned the car as they fled the French officers. These hauls were around $420,000 ($3.9 million in 2022).

Maybe museum directors took comfort in the pieces recovered before the exhibit. Even the Louvre in France decided to lend a highly valuable Cézanne, *The Card Players*, to the show in Aix-en-Provence. The painting was worth one million dollars in 1961. By comparison, *La Tante Marie* was worth $150,000. However, she was still one of the most treasured pieces in the St. Louis museum when loaned to the Pavillon Vendome.[6]

As the art museum prepared to ship the Cézanne to France, another significant theft occurred along the Riviera on July 17, 1961. One late evening, thieves backed a truck up to the museum door, pried off the grill, forced open the lock, and left no fingerprints behind when they removed fifty-seven pieces of art. This was the most sizable hit yet and estimates in 1961 ranged from $1.3 to $2 million.[7] It took place in the small town of Saint-Tropez, at the Annonciade Museum of Modern Art. The museum was a former chapel, isolated in a pine grove, and remained unguarded at night—a perfect target for thieves.

The early string of thefts in France demonstrated the ease with which criminals could steal art. The Pavillon Vendome hosted the Cézanne exhibit that August. Like the chapel in Saint-Tropez, the owner repurposed the Vendome into an art museum.

When the precious artworks of Cézanne arrived in France, they would be in the care of a museum that was just twenty years in the making and not designed to protect treasures. Before converting to a museum, a Catholic girls' boarding school occupied the building until 1941. The museum director lived in the same building as the Cézanne exhibit and cared for the property. This put art directors and private collectors on edge as they prepared to send valuable paintings to the French Riviera, a bed of art thieves.

The French museum amped up its security efforts to ease the fears of their lenders and exhibit staff. A tall stone wall already surrounded the perimeter of the property. They added guards to the single-gated street entrance. The stone museum had three floors, so they situated St. Louis and Paris loans on the second floor as an added safety precaution. Outside the exhibit room, guards stood at the post, and not too far away, the museum director slept on the same floor as the paintings.[8]

Despite the added security, it did not deter the art thieves. The burglars entered the premises in the middle of the night, discreetly away from the view of armed security. They reached the building wall, located the second-floor entrance, and climbed. The men scaled the museum wall until they reached the second-floor window. They cut through the screen, entered the exhibit room, and stripped eight Cézannes from their frames. The guards in the adjoining room and the exhibit's director peacefully slept through the entire heist! The thieves rolled up the pieces, slipped out the way they came, and disappeared.[9]

Men with machine guns stood guard 24/7 outside the museum doors. The front door had a decorative stone relief on each side; both featured the upper torso of a man. In a bit of irony, each figure touched their face, posing in disbelief and anguish, as if the sculptor created them for the exact moment thieves snuck out of the museum under the nose of armed security.

La Tante Marie became the first museum property stolen, and *Nude* became the second. It was another odd coincidence considering they both landed in the museum's collection less than a week apart in 1934.

Word of the theft in France reached the St. Louis museum the following day, August 15, 1961. The museum's director, responding

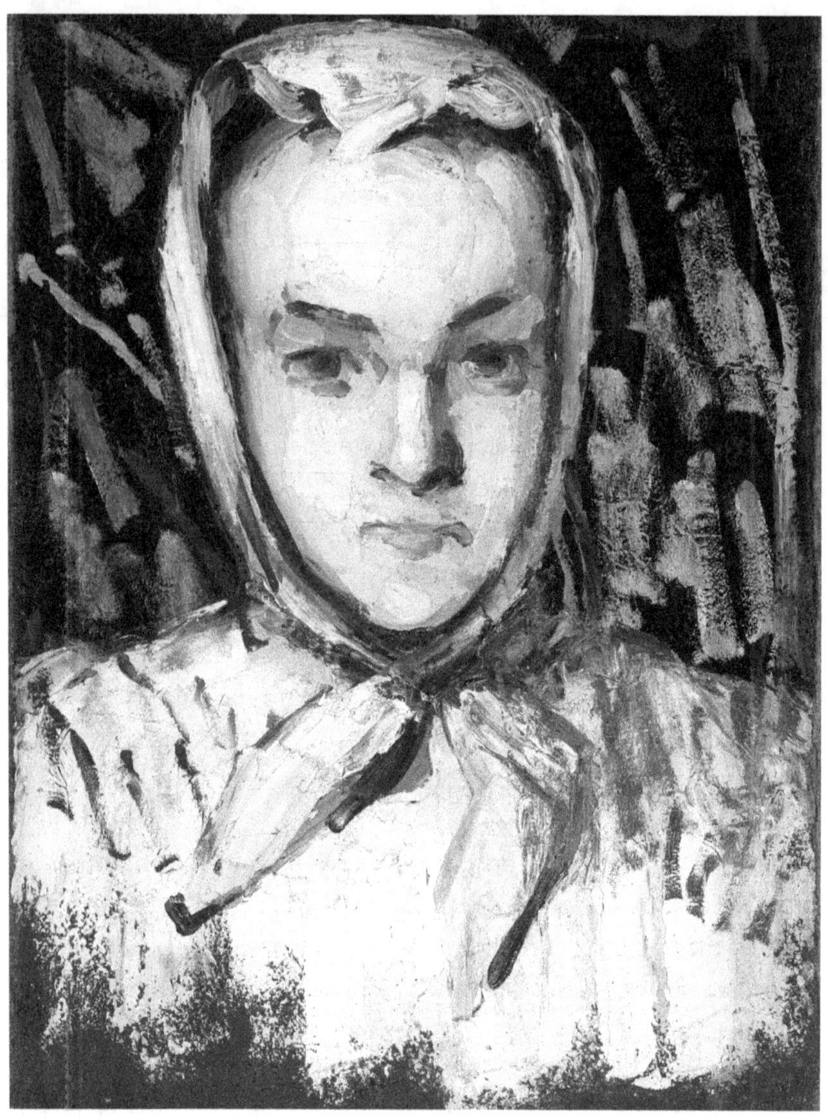

La Tante Marie *(1866-1867), a.k.a.* Marie Cézanne, the Artist's Sister *(recto)*
By Paul Cézanne, French, 1839–1906, oil on canvas; 22 × 15½ inches;
Saint Louis Art Museum, Museum Purchase 34:1934.
Stolen in August 1961 while on loan to a museum in France.
Recovered in April 1962.

to the heist, stated the painting was "lent with some reluctance." Thankfully, the Saint Louis Art Museum sent just one Cézanne in its collection.

The Cézanne heist was part of the earliest stage in the art theft epidemic to spread from Europe to the United States. The eight Cézanne paintings stolen in 1961 made it the most valuable art heist of its time. It was also, quite possibly, the most daring string of robberies on the French Riviera.

The 1960s crime wave in southern France gave birth to multiple millionaire theories of the motives behind stolen art. Soviet upper-class citizens bought stolen art to liquidate their bank accounts to hide their wealth from the Communist government. Wealthy South Americans purchased stolen art to reduce their tax liability.[10] Finally, the most popular theory was the evil, opulent art lover. Imagine a wealthy man who commissions art thieves to steal for his collection. He places the hot masterpiece in a secret room for his eyes only. Much of this speculation still existed a decade later when *Nude* was stolen. In reality, thieves stole art for more practical reasons.

A French gang's criminal scheme to collect ransom money explained the increase in art crime on the French Riviera. Most collectors carried insurance policies on art in case of a loss. A portion of the insurance policy could be used to pay the ransom to get the art back. Insurance companies considered ransom payments a less expensive option than the cost of a claim for a total loss or an investigation to recover the art.

Closely associated with the ransom scheme was the reward scheme. The reward money could be funded through the insurance policy. A reward could encourage art dealers and collectors to be on the lookout; it was also an opportunity to scam the insurance company. Some people stole art just to claim a reward for its return. In this case, the person who located the paintings and collected the reward was involved with the thieves. Within two weeks of the Cézanne exhibit heist, the French museum offered up to $300,000 for the safe return of the Cézanne paintings.[11] Still, several months passed without recovery. The thieves who took the paintings from the exhibit likely considered a reward scheme as a risk for getting caught.

The motivation for the string of art thefts was twofold: weak security and rising values. Thieves took art treasures from chapels, hotels, and chalets with the ease of picking a door or opening a window. One columnist wrote that the boom in art values dwarfed the "climb in stocks, real estate, and other familiar investment mediums."[12]

An international currency expert declared that since 1945, Impressionists and Post-Impressionists were the "blue chips" of paintings, soaring at 2,000 percent in value. He explained that prices rose from 50 percent to 100 percent a year until 1958. The rising popularity of art could have been the source of inspiration for Wilson's idea for the black-tie auction that would further contribute to higher values from this point forward. The compounding issues would sustain art thefts for decades to come.

Museums sought modern masters, and once in their collection, they stayed for the long haul.[13] The remaining inventory for personal art collectors dwindled. It was another reason auctions became a volatile event. The auction stakes eventually made it impossible for museums to compete with the individual wealth of their art patrons. The extraordinary rise in art values became irresistible to thieves, hence the start of the modern-day war on art, rooted in southern France.

Eight months passed before police found the stolen Cézanne paintings in an abandoned car in Marseille. On April 10, 1962, thieves left the eight oil-painted canvases rolled up together and across the back seat. If the French museum's insurance paid a ransom to thieves for the return, they kept it quiet. Acknowledging the ransom payment in the press would only encourage more thefts.

La Tante Marie safely returned to the City Art Museum of St. Louis. The museum sent the painting off to an expert in Kansas City for restoration. The frame was missing, and her edges were slightly frayed, but she escaped significant damage. The canvas was 21¾ × 15 inches. A few spots of the liner on the painting's backside were torn, so the museum director and restorer agreed to replace it. The original liner strengthened the picture and prepared it for sale decades earlier.

Peeling away the layers of glue and yellowed varnish beneath the liner, the restorer began to see the image of a peasant woman emerge. She turned out to be Cézanne's mother. A theft in Aix-en-Provence, the birthplace of Cézanne, bore a painting of his mother in an ironic twist of fate.

Cézanne painted his mother two years before Marie. As a young, thrifty artist, he reused the backside of his canvas to paint his sister in 1866.[14] *La Tante Marie* returned to the city's museum a month later and was displayed for public viewing. Visitors could see *The Artist's Mother (verso)* in a dual-sided frame. With the new discovery, the value increased *La Tante Marie* by another $75,000 in 1962.[15] It had to be one of the rarest ever conclusions to an art theft.

The art museum vowed to revisit its lending policy, but it would not be enough. Art investigators across the world dealt with an epidemic proportion of thefts. For Europe, the losses amounted to $200 million by 1969 (i.e., $1.5 billion in 2022). Federal investigators estimated the value of stateside thefts as also high, though without a central deposit to track stolen art, no figure accurately described the devastation.[16]

No art database nor a reasonable method of communication existed between investigating agencies across multiple cities at this time. Therefore, the recovery rate was an abysmal 20 percent. After five years, the odds of recovery almost plummeted to the chances of winning the Powerball jackpot.

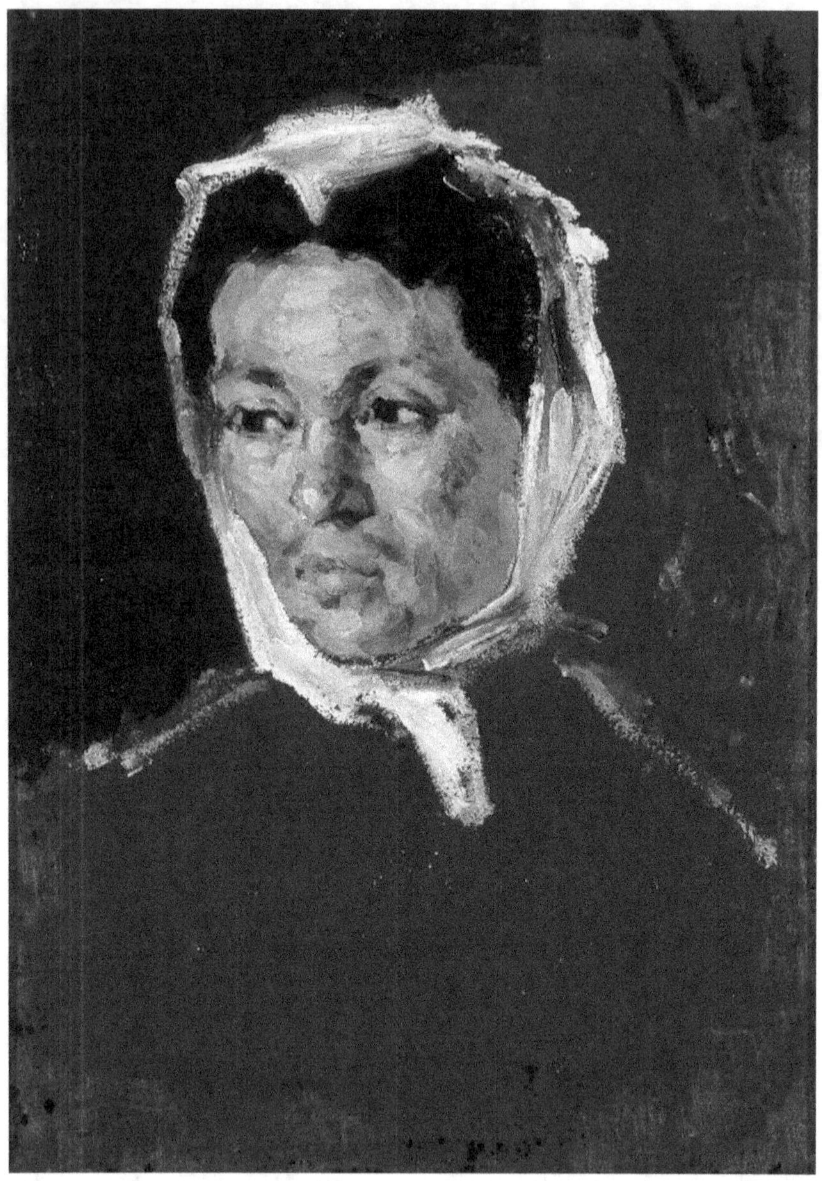

The Artist's Mother *(verso), discovered on the backside of* La Tante Marie/
Marie Cézanne, the Artist's Sister *(recto) during restoration in 1962.*

Art thefts were on the verge of an epidemic in the States. The artist's sister and mother faced the same security risks on Art Hill as on the French Riviera. Art could be stolen anywhere, even in St. Louis and in the presence of museum guards and one intimidating bronze man with a big sword and a horse. *Nude* was the first to prove how easy it could be in 1973.

There was one more secret about the theft only to be learned years later. The public was unaware the Corsican Mafia stole *La Tante Marie* in 1961 as part of the gang's string of heists along the French Riviera. The act may have even inspired the epidemic of art thefts that followed in America. Any theory about missing art should look at all of the usual suspects historically attached to art crimes.

The Corsican gang ravaged France of their art, and the Sicilian Mafia had pilfered unprotected art in Italy. In America, the most powerful mafia during the 1960s and 1970s was La Cosa Nostra, also known as the American Mafia. The three criminal operations worked together to bring heroin to the United States for decades. But could they have also shared a scheme for stealing art?

The Art of Organized Crime

INVESTIGATING AGENCIES provided the same theories behind the Cézanne heist and the *Nude* theft in 1973. A decade of art thefts had passed without progress in identifying a significant force behind art crimes.

Scotland Yard investigators believed it to be an art ring. They described the thieves as a highly organized group with a diverse skill set under the leadership of a cultured thief and an unscrupulous art dealer. The French police believed gangs perpetrated the thefts along the French Riviera robberies. The French police also admitted they knew more about smuggling drugs through an international network than smuggling art.

Rome's Minister for the Recovery of Works of Art was the most seasoned investigator. He successfully returned over 2,500 paintings and other objects from Germany since WWII, taken during Hitler's massive plunder. He believed the big player in the underground art market was the same that helped Nazis smuggle and fence art.[1]

This subtle reference was likely to Martin Fabiani, an art dealer and member of the Corsican Mafia, flagged on numerous lists for his dealings in Nazi-looted art in France. (Fabiani was the executor of Vollard's art collection after Vollard was killed in a suspicious car accident in 1939.)

In a way, they were all on the right track. Decades would pass before experts attributed the Cézanne heist in France to the Corsican Mafia. From the 1960s to the 1970s, the Corsican gang also became known for the "French Connection" narcotics operation. The racket was responsible for 80 percent of heroin smuggled into America. Once in the country, the American Mafia illegally distributed the highly addictive substance throughout their network of cities. Eventually, art would get tied up in the scheme as black market currency.

In 1969, the Sicilian Mafia stole a highly valuable painting from the church of San Lorenzo in Palermo, Italy. The Italian government was going after La Cosa Nostra (LCN),[2] the most infamous organized crime operation in Italy, and perhaps the world.

About the same time Mario Puzo authored *The Godfather*, the federal government changed its lexicon from the Mafia to organized crime Syndicate. The new description accurately reflected the American melting pot of criminals and gangs working together for more considerable control of legal businesses and illegal vices.

The Sicilian LCN played a significant role in the American evolution of organized crime. The period's largest and most dangerous organized crime network in the United States was sometimes referred to as just Cosa Nostra or the American Mafia.

Unfortunately, the puzzle pieces that pointed to organized crime did not come fully together for the FBI until the latter part of the 1970s. Foreign art investigators closed in on the perpetrator fleecing Europe. But the FBI had no similar art recovery team to tackle stateside thefts. Perhaps more embarrassing was the federal government had spent excess resources to take down organized crime while the Syndicate may have pilfered art under its nose.

If the museum almost lost its Cézanne to the Corsican Mafia in France, then perhaps they lost their Picasso to organized crime in St. Louis. Though the FBI had chased organized crime since the days of Prohibition an extra effort to crack down on American organized crime started around the late 1960s and early 1970s. The US Department of Justice (DOJ) put special task forces in place in numerous cities to eliminate organized crime, and it coincided with the double-digit growth of art thefts.

I began investigating the idea that organized criminals might have stole *Nude* in 1973. At the time of the robbery, I was just a kid and knew absolutely nothing about organized crime. Everything I knew as an adult came from the movies. Since Hollywood had already distorted the public's perception of art thieves, I decided it was best to ignore what I learned through Martin Scorsese's films.

The short version of the Mafia's history in the States showed a membership of primarily Sicilian heritage, which expanded to Italian heritage. The LCN operation expanded its rackets across multiple US cities and towns. To do so, they often formed alliances or gained the cooperation of local hoodlums. The melting pot of ethnic gang operations and perhaps the most notable alliances between Italian and Jewish mobsters became the basis for perpetuating the idea of a National Crime Syndicate (a.k.a. Syndicate). For clarity, the Syndicate would be the whole network of cooperating criminals, not just LCN.

However, in the 1970s, the heart of the federal government's focus was on the LCN because they were the most powerful criminal operation in America. I located some information to help sort out exactly what the DOJ's perception of "organized crime" had been at the time criminals were stealing art in the 1970s.

The US government compared the Mafia structure in the 1970s to the organization chart of a large corporation. They have their own governing laws "rigidly enforced," explains one federal document. The DOJ further expressed that organized crime entailed intricate conspiracies carried out over many years to gain control over a "whole field of activity to amass huge profits."[3]

LCN was the Syndicate's largest and most dangerous body. It ran like a typical business structure, and the LCN crime commission provided leadership at the top. The commission included bosses from at least five crime families. The DOJ identified twenty-four crime families located in major cities across the States, each having a local crime boss. Each family worked with and often controlled weaker organized crime groups operating in its town. The layered operation protected the leaders, the network, and the scheme.

The federal government depicted the LCN in a traditional company organizational chart to demonstrate the operation hierarchy within each city. At the top, a crime boss ruled the territory with his underboss as second-in-command. The consigliere was the advisor to the boss. The underboss was in charge of the next layer, the capos (or lieutenants). The capos oversaw the criminal scheme and gave orders to the "soldiers," who were at the bottom of the LCN ranks. The soldiers carried out orders from leaders, typically including threats, assault, murder, and enforcing discipline among members and nonmembers.

The lowest layer of the organized crime chart was the nonmember associates or other overlapping criminal organizations that advanced the Mafia's rackets. This could be a criminal so far removed from the network they didn't know who pulled the strings.

The lowest-level players were not always criminals. Some were just victims forced into participation through extortion and intimidation. Someone owning a legal company might be threatened into cooperation, allowing members of the Mafia to exploit the business for money laundering or some other scheme.

The DOJ summarized the Mafia strategy for making money as, "They used monopolization, terrorism, extortion and tax evasion to drive out lawful ownership and leadership and to exact illegal profits from the public"[4]

For any racket to work, corruption was a key ingredient to the livelihood of organized crime. The Mafia infiltrated government offices, political positions, law enforcement, and labor unions. The President's Commission on organized crime reported in 1967 that corruption payments were the Mafia's biggest expense.

Organized crime became a parasite, leeching onto legal businesses and government offices to further its schemes. The LCN's preferred legal fronts to launder money and evade taxes included produce stands, real estate, vending companies, restaurants, taverns, and labor unions. The most popular illegal schemes during the 1960s and 1970s were gambling, narcotics, extortion, loan sharking, and labor racketeering.

I could not help but notice that "theft" did not make the top list of schemes. The DOJ looked at theft as a secondary activity for the Mafia, an engagement thought only to be a byproduct of other rackets. For example, the LCN had a stronghold on labor unions, including the most powerful, the Teamsters Union, which gave them inside information on cargo and transportation shipments. A theft ring might pay the Mafia for information on a load of goods to plan and execute a heist.

In 1976, the DOJ released a separate guide on combatting the growing theft and fencing problem. The timing was not only relative to the St. Louis art thefts, it provided characteristics that would differentiate a Syndicate-operated fencing scheme from all others. Generally, the heists operated sporadically, and the targeted goods were high-value, low-volume items: jewelry, antiques, and art.

According to the DOJ, if the presence of organized crime existed in a city with a professional fencing operation, it likely involved the Syndicate. Otherwise, it could be a stand-alone operation—still organized crime—but not necessarily under the Mafia's control.

Unfortunately, the police guidance came three years after someone robbed the art museum of the Rose Period Picasso.

When art thefts began to explode in the States, the government had a concerted effort to eliminate organized crime. The American Mafia might have stolen art just as their familial faction had done in Sicily in 1969 while under the same type of pressure. In fact, federal heat started in eight major Mafia cities in the same year. Eventually, it would expand to more, and coincidentally, so would the increase in art thefts in the United States.

DOJ TURNS UP THE HEAT

By the time President John F. Kennedy appointed his brother Robert F. Kennedy (RFK) as Attorney General (AG) in 1961, organized crime had flourished. RFK was appalled at the enormity in which organized crime grew. During his term, he increased pressure on the FBI to pursue and convict organized crime members and associates.

Jimmy Hoffa, a famous and influential Teamsters Union leader, considered to be under the direct influence of the Mafia, became RFK's number one nemesis. The Syndicate played an integral role in Hoffa's rise, and the government was well aware of the connection. Hoffa fell out of favor with the LCN while in prison (jailed for mail fraud and racketeering). Once released, he attempted to regain his position but disappeared permanently in 1975.

After Hoffa lost his position, the Syndicate maintained control of several unions. Union employees' pension funds became the Mafia's bankroll. They invested pension money into real estate, specifically Las Vegas hotels and casinos.

The pressure did not go away when Kennedy left the AG office in 1964. When he became a US senator, he led the efforts to develop a structured, focused action against organized crime. In November 1967, under the advisement of AG Ramsey Clark, the DOJ created a new unit dedicated to taking down organized crime. Kennedy did not live to see the operation come to fruition. A lone assassin killed RFK in June 1968, just five years after his brother and two months after Martin Luther King, Jr. died under similar circumstances.

The Organized Crime Strike Force (OCSF) officially launched in eight major Syndicate cities in 1969. The cities were Brooklyn, Boston, Buffalo*, Chicago*, Detroit*, Miami, Newark* and Philadelphia* (*the location of the LCN commission of crime families in 1973).[5] The OCSF had various skilled members to break up criminal organizations, but an expert in art theft was not one of them. A single OCSF team included US prosecutors and government agents from the FBI, IRS, and Customs. The team navigated obscure law violations and various avenues of financial fraud to put the clamp on Mafia cash flow.

Shortly after OCSF was established, the Racketeer Influenced and Corrupt Organizations (RICO) Act became law in 1970. The government designed the law to prosecute people engaged in organized crime. For it to apply to a crime, the federal government must prove the defendant engaged in more than one racketeering activity. Additionally, the RICO Act states they must have "directly invested in, maintained an interest in, or participated in a criminal enterprise affecting interstate or foreign commerce."

The law helped federal agents arrest Syndicate members. Still, fully prosecuting and putting criminals behind bars was often challenging, resulting in small jail sentences, if any. The feds pressured the Syndicate, and like their criminal brethren in Italy and Corsica, they turned to a new scheme: stealing art. It was easy to steal, worth a lot of money, and a discreet currency to conduct illegal business while under the FBI's thumb. Organized crime was barely on the agency's radar for stealing art in 1973.

The pressure on organized crime continued with the Federal Conspiracy Law (1977), which made it a crime if two or more people engaged in an agreement to commit a crime and at least one of the criminals took at least one step toward the scheme. Whereas the RICO Act focused on a crime committed, the conspiracy law only needed evidence of someone advancing a scheme. The law could then focus on the broader layers of criminals involved in racketeering schemes, including theft.

The new conspiracy law did not exist when *Nude* disappeared. Weak, stolen property laws in 1973 also made it difficult to prosecute anyone purchasing or selling stolen property. Law enforcement had to practically catch a thief in the act of stealing to get a conviction, so to bust a fence selling stolen property was a bigger hurdle. Agents went undercover as interested buyers to catch a fence selling goods. The tactic was only prosecutable if the fence acknowledged the items as stolen to the undercover agents.

The environment seemed ripe for an art theft racket. The Syndicate usually used unregulated markets and legal loopholes to operate their schemes. Missouri just happened to be one of the states where stolen property laws favored the criminal.

In 1976, a retired high-ranking New York police official cited stolen art as the "ideal way for organized crime to move money, to pay off heroin shipments." He explained that no customs officer would ask questions about a rolled-up painting.[6] It seems he was on the right track, suggesting that the Syndicate used art as collateral in the underworld for illegal goods and services.

The question remained was organized crime present in the Gateway City? If so, was there a motive to steal art, and was there a network capable of successfully profiting from the act?

MISSOURI AND ORGANIZED CRIME

The term "Mafia" brings to mind visions of burly, East Coast men with that New York-Sicilian brogue portrayed in the movies. The thought of a "mafioso" using St. Louis slang crossed my mind: "Horseshoe Jimmy just got blown up on hwy 55, or was it hwy *farty-far* [forty-four]? You know, about a *'quarder*-mile' from the exit to Imo's." (Only someone familiar with the local dialect could appreciate the interpretation.) All kidding aside, Missouri really had an organized crime problem, and car bombs happened more frequently than most other cities.

The statewide corruption and the Syndicate role came to a head in the 1970s, timing that aligned with the wave of local art thefts. It began with a Missouri task force study on organized crime that focused on Syndicate operations in St. Louis, Kansas City, and rural towns with links to the Mafia.

The gang on the west side of the state was nicknamed the Kansas City Outfit due to its close ties with the Chicago Outfit, the Mafia of Al "Scarface" Capone, who died in 1947. The research considered Kansas City a more robust criminal operation than St. Louis. The report indicated the Kansas City crime family's primary source of income was "theft."[7] Nevertheless, I found no museum art thefts in Kansas City archives from the era.

The report assessed the local St. Louis LCN as having less power than their Interstate 70 brethren. St. Louis had three factions, which might have added to the perception of a division of power. In reality, the three groups had just formed an alliance, moving the LCN crime boss to the top.

East St. Louis also had close ties to the Chicago Outfit. The East Side crime boss, Frank "Buster" Wortman, had ruled the rackets on the Metro East, southern Illinois, and southern Missouri for almost thirty years. Arthur Berne took over the rackets after Wortman's death in 1968, reporting as a lieutenant in the Chicago Outfit and under the authority of Chicago dons Joey "Doves" Auippa and John "Jackie the Lackey" Cerone through the 1970s.[8] Berne's East Side operation in the 1970s was just one of the local organized criminal factions. But he was not the highest-ranking officer in the St. Louis Syndicate operation. The St. Louis LCN crime family held the higher hand locally during the time of the art thefts.

The local LCN crime family had roots in multiple Prohibition gangs, but all of Sicilian or Italian heritage. In the 1970s, Anthony "Tony G" Giordano headed the St. Louis crime family. His control of a local towing company contracted with the city police starting in 1969 was just one of the multiple infiltrations into city government. Violence, extortion, and political corruption plagued the local vending industry, a local mob monopoly for decades.

A third faction operated on the South Side of St. Louis, referred to as the Syrian Mafia and an alliance of the LCN. They were an evolution of the Prohibition gang, the Cuckoos. The name allegedly came from Al Capone describing the gangsters as a bunch of "cuckoos" who kept knocking off his Italian gangsters sent to expand Capone's bootlegging territory to St. Louis. The revised name became the Syrian Mafia, though I was confused by the lack of Syrian surnames in the gang. Like the other gangs, they profited from gambling rackets and labor racketeering. Their longtime crime boss was James "Horseshoe Jimmy" Michaels.[9] And yes, he died in a car bomb on hwy 55.

With the St. Louis territory overlap of the three gangs, bloody criminal conflicts or mutual cooperation ruled the area. However, by 1969, these factions formed an alliance.[10] The crime coalition was likely a reaction to the increasing pressure the feds put on organized crime, combined with the passing of the guard on the East Side. In the 1970s, the LCN crime boss oversaw all local organized crime operations, according to multiple news reports.

The 1970 research project into Missouri organized crime may have helped justify a federally funded task force to combat organized crime. President Nixon planned to expand the OCSF from the original eight cities to eighteen, including St. Louis and Kansas City.[11] Regardless of what the 1970 report said, some officials denied the presence of organized crime in St. Louis, including Mayor Alfonso Cervantes. He publicly stated, "I know of no organized crime in the city," despite the results that identified three organized crime factions working together in St. Louis.[12]

According to the defunct *St. Louis Globe-Democrat* (January 1971), the study's results showed the St. Louis underworld engaged in labor racketeering, narcotics traffic, gambling, loan sharking, and infiltration of legitimate businesses. This seemed consistent with most of the news reports from the period.

St. Louis's organized crime history goes back to Prohibition. Once Prohibition ended, criminals either left the area or joined the remaining gangs. A clear organized crime presence existed in the archived newspaper reports from the period. Violence, gambling, extortion, prostitution, and drug trafficking attached to organized crime existed into the 1970s. The St. Louis mayor was either in denial, misunderstood the extent of the problem, or was under the Mafia's influence.

St. Louis and Kansas City Syndicate operations had ties to each other. Both worked closely with the Chicago Outfit, and St. Louis LCN also had direct relations with the crime family of Detroit, Michigan, known as the Detroit Partnership. By the time the St. Louis art thefts started, the three factions in the St. Louis metropolitan area were under the control of the local LCN crime boss.

Missouri-organized crime factions had corrupted multiple labor unions. At the center of this connection was another local St. Louisan and prominent attorney, Morris Shenker. The criminal defense lawyer had a national reputation for successfully defending criminal bosses against federal racketeering and tax evasion charges. He was the chief counsel for Hoffa when he was president of the Teamsters Union and continued to be involved after Hoffa's departure.

The headline on the cover of *Life* magazine, May 29, 1970, came at a time the OCSF had newly expanded to St. Louis. The article, titled "Investigative Report: St. Louis: The Mayor, the Mob and the Lawyer," alleged the corruption of Mayor Cervantes and prominent defense attorney Shenker.[13]

The article alleged Shenker controlled $700 million in pension funds and investments, mainly going to Las Vegas properties. Shenker was scrutinized for his connection to organized crime figures and investments in the Dunes Hotel and Casino in Las Vegas. The FBI believed the casino was operating under mob authority and skimming money. For at least nineteen years, the feds chased Shenker for an indictment, and when they finally got one, he was eighty-nine and deemed too old and ill to stand trial.

Cervantes selected a highly regarded criminal defense lawyer for the mob to oversee the crime problem in St. Louis. The St. Louis mayor appointed Shenker to Chairman of the Committee on Crime and Law Enforcement, starting January 1, 1970. The selection only added to the growing suspicion of the mayor having a close relationship with local organized crime leaders. Cervantes's definition of crime had to be street crime, not organized crime. After all, in his opinion, organized crime did not exist in his city.

Cervantes was serving his fifth year as St. Louis mayor when *Life* magazine's exposé referred to him as a "steady liaison of the St. Louis Underworld." The article accused him of consorting with local Mafia members while serving as mayor. The report presented multiple financial ties to the exact criminal figures before his mayoral position. However, Cervantes continued to deny connections to any of them.

The *Life* reporter identified the mayor's first campaign manager, a son-in-law of the Syrian Mafia boss, as the liaison to local Mafia leadership. Both Cervantes and Shenker sued *Life* magazine for libel and lost their cases. This became Cervantes's last term as mayor. After leaving office, he would lead an effort beginning in 1974 to revitalize the real estate district of the Maryland Plaza mall area in Central West End of St. Louis city.

Shenker continued to be under the bureau's watch for his connection to real estate investments, which used pension funds. A couple of years after the *Life* exposé, a local report said Shenker received a $500,000 finder's fee for the real estate purchase of the Aladdin Hotel and gambling casino in Las Vegas.

Shenker originally selected three Detroit investors whose licenses "were denied by the Nevada Gaming Control Board because of their connections with organized crime leaders and hoodlums."[14] The final investors in the Aladdin property included the deputy of the St. Louis city's license collector office.[15] Not too surprising since the deputy's boss, the city license collector, also accepted bribes to further the local vending monopoly racket the Mafia controlled. *The Los Angeles Times* reported the hotel as a mob resort. The Aladdin comped rooms, meals, and liquor to twenty underworld figures, including figures from St. Louis, Detroit, Kansas City, and New York.[16]

Though Shenker and Cervantes were not associated with the local art thefts, they did represent the level of Mafia corruption in St. Louis from the period. If local organized crime infiltrated high-profile positions, it could have easily reached less notable roles, including security staff at a city-owned museum.

By the end of 1972, the extent of corruption in Missouri was boldly on display. Lt. Governor William S. Morris (then acting governor for Warren E. Hearnes) pardoned East Side criminal Berne. The pardon "restored full citizenship rights," and removed Berne's three felony convictions in Missouri from his record. Additionally, the acting governor pardoned two Kansas City Mafia members in the last days before the newly elected governor stepped into his role.[17]

Any doubt that the Mafia existed in St. Louis vanished after locating numerous reports of organized crime activity in the city during the 1970s. The media reported on underworld figures and organized crime schemes, mostly gambling, labor racketeering, narcotics, extortion, and corruption.

The St. Louis Mafia monopolized vending companies to evade taxes and launder money through a legal business. But their control also benefited the New York Mafia, who secured contracts to service major sports venues across thirty states under a single corporation.[18]

When the Picasso went missing in 1973, the St. Louis and Detroit Mafia bosses were appealing a federal conviction for concealing to hide their ownership in the Frontier Hotel and Casino in Las Vegas. They lost the appeal in 1974 and finally began serving their sentences in 1975 at a federal prison. Coincidentally, Giordano, the reputed St. Louis crime boss, was released for good behavior in late 1977, returning to St. Louis just six weeks before the last set of Saint Louis Art Museum robberies.

Giordano returned from prison, sick with cancer, and his imminent death would signal the final decline of the local Mafia. The *St. Louis Post-Dispatch* reported the criminal résumé of Giordano after he lost his battle with the disease in 1980. The story read like a tribute to "the man," subtly reflecting the newspaper's own loss of a central figure in their criminal reports through the last decade of his life.[19]

He was an international heroin smuggler for the Mafia before rising to the position of local crime boss. He brought drugs from Italy to distribute from the Midwest to the East Coast and directly worked alongside notorious mobsters Frank Costello and Lucky Luciano.[20] After scouring years of old organized crime stories, the criminal eulogy said the Mafia leader was also known for "fencing of stolen goods."

The local LCN demonstrated a consistent ability to cooperate in a network of criminal organizations. Moving stolen art from one Syndicate city to another was not outside their capabilities. When federal agencies began to squelch local mafia operations, the financial losses may have sparked the motive to steal art and *Nude* could have been the first victim.

7
CHAPTER

The Art of Fencing

ART MUSEUMS ARE TYPICALLY NONPROFIT, and galleries are often for-profit businesses. When artwork enters the museum's hands, it is typically the last stop of ownership. On the other hand, art galleries are a place for private art collectors to buy works of well-known artists. Museums and galleries share a love for art and a common source of pain…the art thief.

Nude was the city's first museum theft of a painting, but *Russian School Children* might have been the city's first gallery oil painting to be stolen. Two months after the Picasso painting vanished from the museum wall, a Rockwell oil painting also disappeared at the hands of a thief.

From 1973 to 1977, thieves targeted one particular gallery on multiple occasions in St. Louis: Arts International, located in Clayton Municipality of St. Louis County. The gallery was part of a chain of galleries that Jacob Sachs* owned in Chicago, New York, and New Orleans. The gallery's headquarters were in Chicago, leaving daily operations at the Clayton branch to a local manager. The building was located on Maryland Avenue, just three miles west of the City Art Museum. The street was a popular shopping area that boasted opulent jewelry and antique shops. This also made it a hot spot for local thieves.

The gallery featured various exhibits at different times of the year. Norman Rockwell was a favorite theme. Sachs had an exclusive license for Rockwell reprints and often displayed Rockwell lithographs. In June of 1973, the gallery exhibited a Rockwell oil painting, *Russian School Children.*

Russian School Children was the only Rockwell oil painting for sale in the States when featured at the 1973 summer exhibit in Clayton. Sachs acquired the painting from Danenberg Galleries, which dealt with original Rockwell paintings, in New York City sometime before 1973.

For decades, Rockwell's art did not carry the stature of Picasso's art, though they both produced work during the same century. Rockwell's art depicted American life and was often reproduced into calendars, greeting cards, and other collectibles.

Publishers commissioned Rockwell's works, and most of them graced the cover of *The Saturday Evening Post.* The artist was just twenty-two years old when he painted his first cover for the *Post* and produced 321 covers over his forty-seven-year career with the magazine. He had become the most recognized artist in America.[1]

As the *Post* dwindled in popularity, Rockwell left the magazine in 1963 and began producing illustrations for *Look* magazine. *Look* was the second most popular magazine, just behind *Life* magazine and in front of the *Post.* During his time at *Look,* Rockwell's paintings contained more controversial scenes than at the *Post,* though his style was irrefutably recognizable.

The US and the USSR were in the midst of the Cold War. The October 3, 1967 edition of *Look* focused on Russia, fifty years after its revolution. The magazine photographed a Rockwell painting, *Russian School Children,* for the magazine article. It was perhaps the most *un-American* American painting he had produced in his career.

The painting featured a classroom of Russian children sitting at their desks, eyes forward, and attentive to the lesson being taught. They wore the color red, showing from underneath their shirts, a hue that represented the Communist government. A bust of Vladimir Lenin sat at the head of the classroom.

Rockwell's art was quickly becoming an investment worth owning. *Russian School Children* was the main exhibit feature at Arts International in June 1973. A St. Louis businessman and avid art collector purchased the painting for $25,000 shortly before the show's start in June.[2] He agreed to keep the artwork on display during the exhibit, advertised to end on July 6, 1973. The picture was six years old and was quickly appreciating in value.

In the early morning hours of June 25, an eyewitness saw a man exit the Clayton gallery with a framed picture in hand. The robber smashed the front door's glass, went inside the gallery, bypassed all other works, and stole *Russian School Children*. He carried the piece, still enclosed in its 2 × 4-foot dull gold-white molded frame, into his car and fled.[3]

The Rockwell theft came just two months after someone took *Nude* from the art museum, though their departures were starkly different, much like the artists' careers. Picasso's career showed a diverse style, often described in distinctive periods. A Rose Period Picasso looked nothing like his Cubism period. Norman Rockwell's art was easily identifiable and had a consistent style of work over the decades. Rockwell created abundant art during his lifetime, primarily for commercial publication purposes. However, no artist was more prolific than Picasso, who made over 13,500 paintings, among thousands of other creations, in his lifetime.

The timing of the two heists was relatively close, occurring in April and June, respectively. The differences between the two heists could reflect different thieves at work or the same thief adjusting to two very different circumstances.

In 1973, the city's art museum was not conducive to a smash-and-grab. It featured just two entrances, and guards secured both 24/7. The better plan was blending in as a museum guest and leaving with the Picasso under the nose of daytime security.

The Clayton gallery was small by comparison and used an alarm system to guard the art treasures after business hours. This made the smash-and-grab approach the most efficient strategy to take the Rockwell.

Russian School Children appeared to be a good investment, doubling its value immediately. The gallery reimbursed the businessman for the total purchase price. He was reasonably upset when he learned the piece was valued closer to $40,000.[4] The decision to let the gallery continue to display the painting probably made the loss sting much more.

The insurance company reimbursed the Clayton gallery $20,000, the amount recorded on the insurance policy at the time of theft. The $5,000 profit Sachs made from the original sale to a local collector was gone like the painting.

In recent years, the former assistant director at the gallery recalled a private investigator who found *Russian School Children* in 1973. The detective advised leaving the case alone, as the thieves who took it were dangerous and likely to steal it again if recovered.[5]

ROCKWELL REAPPEARS, TWICE

Stolen art rarely resurfaced in the open market in the same city it was stolen in. Stories of theft mostly faded over the months and may have never reached a buyer in another market. Time and relocation of the art made it reasonably easy for anyone to sell it into the open market. The case of the stolen Rockwell was one of those stories.

The protocol for stolen art included a brief description and picture circulated among local law enforcement. Typically, members of the Art Dealers Association of America (ADAA) reported thefts at their galleries and museums. The ADAA limited the distribution of stolen art announcements to members. They eventually expanded the distribution list to nonmembers. Still, there was no immediate way to verify the number of dealers who received notifications about the 1973 St. Louis art thefts.

Media communication sources provided a medium for notifying the public, though it was short-lived. A gallery heist doesn't carry the weight of a museum robbery, so the local newspapers buried the story of the Rockwell theft inside their pages.

The stolen Picasso and the Rockwell would have been on the FBI's radar. However, only the local FBI office maintained records of the theft. Art theft required a better solution, but it did not come until 1979 when the FBI launched the National Stolen Art File (NSAF).

The NSAF was a collection of art thefts reported to the FBI, allowing the entire agency to record and view information on stolen art in any US city. This included previous robberies from local areas with a minimal value of $2,000 and the artwork to be of a reputable artist. Investigating agencies were required to report stolen and recovered art to maintain accuracy.[6]

The stolen Rockwell and Picasso would have easily met the requirements to have them listed in the NSAF. Nevertheless, human error proved problematic. Not all the stolen art cases transitioned from local files to the NSAF. And not all the art recovered would make it off the NSAF list.

The FBI relaunched the NSAF in the early 2000s as an internet-friendly, free, public searchable database. It has helped the FBI recover over $800 million in stolen art. In contrast, others, like Art Loss Register, required specific credentials, or a credit card, to list or find art. Art theft victims should have been pleased with the new NSAF, which exposed stolen art to millions of viewers.

However, *Nude* was missing from the new FBI database, whereas the Rockwell was listed in great detail. The site showed *Russian School Children* as stolen in 1973 from the Clayton gallery and listed its alternative names: *Russian Schoolroom* and *Russian Classroom.* There was just one small problem…

THE ROAD TO HOLLYWOOD

George Lucas and Steven Spielberg teamed up for some of the most iconic adventure movies, including *Indiana Jones.* As soon as Lucas could afford them, he bought Norman Rockwell illustrations. Spielberg would follow close behind. As filmmakers, they developed an affinity for the commercial artist and the sweet American moments Rockwell captured in his paintings and illustrations. The critics did not always view Rockwell's work with the esteem of Picasso or Cézanne, but the nostalgic images from the *Saturday Evening Post* struck a chord with the dynamic duo of adventure films. Between them, they built quite a collection.[7]

Perhaps on the heels of the success of the third installment of *Indiana Jones*, Steven Spielberg celebrated with a new painting. He purchased *Russian School Children* for $200,000 in 1989 from a female art dealer in New York specializing in American illustrators. The artwork grew at an approximate 13 percent CAGR between 1973 and 1989.

After having it for seventeen years, Spielberg was shocked to learn he had a stolen Rockwell in his possession, at least according to the FBI website. Once discovered, Spielberg did just what Indiana Jones would have done in this predicament: He contacted the FBI.[8]

The FBI contacted Sachs. Sachs was the owner of *Russian School Children,* according to the record in the FBI database. Learning the news, Sachs expected the FBI to return the painting, but that did not happen. In response to the delay, Sachs initiated a lawsuit against the FBI and Spielberg in 2007 to get *Russian School Children* back.[9]

The problem? The NSAF erroneously listed the painting as missing and set off a chain of legal proceedings that lasted for at least five years. The NY art dealer who sold Spielberg the Rockwell in 1989 stepped into the lawsuit in 2007 to replace Spielberg and faced litigation for ownership. She gave Spielberg another Rockwell painting of similar value, *Peace Corps in Ethiopia*. In exchange, she claimed ownership of *Russian School Children.*

Before selling it to Spielberg, she acquired *Russian School Children* in an auction a year earlier. She purchased it from the Louisiana Purchase Auction held at the Goldberg Auction Gallery of New Orleans in the fall of 1988. Only months before the auction, a Goldberg representative from the gallery offered to sell her *Russian School Children* directly.[10] She scoffed at the $100,000 price tag, stating it was too high. With no takers at that price, the painting soon went on the auction block, and she would get a chance to purchase it for a lower price.

The Goldberg Auction Gallery was not a Sotheby's or Christie's auction house. Without the marketing hype and bidding pressure, buyers had less competition and a chance of getting a good deal.

As a standard practice, the auction advertised the sale in trade magazines and listed the painting in Goldberg's catalog, a catalog that was routinely distributed to hundreds of buyers who could be interested in the auction. Promoting a Rockwell among the auction goods would have been a worthy investment for the gallery and common practice. Auction houses get a commission off the final sale price, commonly between 10 and 15 percent.

The NY art dealer spent time investigating the provenance of the piece. She researched similar works to understand the market value and what was a fair yet responsible offer.[11] The due diligence of both the potential buyer and the auction house protects everyone from liabilities that could arise if the piece turns out to be stolen property, forged, or of questionable provenance.

An unscrupulous art dealer would ignore the procedures and sell it discreetly to someone who may or may not be aware of its shady past. Basically, the same method likely placed *Russian School Children* in the hands of the couple who brought it to the New Orleans auction house in 1988. However, a legit sale of stolen art in an auction requires the last legal owner to authorize and clear its title to go on the auction block.

When the couple brought it to the Goldberg Auction Gallery, fifteen years had passed since it went missing from St. Louis. No one can be sure of the exact path it took from St. Louis to New Orleans, though the thief that took it and perhaps the couple that put it up for auction likely had some answers.

According to a string of FBI communications, Sachs contacted the New York City FBI office to alert them of *Russian School Children's* reemergence in New Orleans in 1988. He saw the Goldberg auction advertisement for the Rockwell painting. The NYC field office passed the information to the St. Louis FBI. St. Louis agents attempted to collect all documents pertaining to the theft, even though they could not locate the original 1973 police report.

The St. Louis office then forwarded the information to the New Orleans FBI field office. The FBI in New Orleans investigated the background of Morton's gallery and verified the painting was still in the gallery's possession. They planned to seize the picture on the day of the auction and waited for the final word from the St. Louis office to move forward.[12]

Meanwhile, Sachs and his lawyers contacted the Goldberg gallery to get the painting back through direct negotiations. The gallery demanded proof of ownership. Neither he nor the insurance company could come up with a receipt of sale or something similar to satisfy the request. This may have influenced Sachs to clear the title and sell it at auction.

He released the FBI from further action in seizing the art in 1988.[13] The Morton Goldberg Auction Gallery sold *Russian School Children* for a final auction price of $70,400. According to the court's evidence, multiple parties agreed to split the auction proceeds. The insurance company received $20,000, the amount of the insurance claim paid to Sachs in 1973. The auction house received 10 percent of the final price as a sales commission.

The couple that brought *Russian School Children* to auction split the balance 50/50 with Sachs. Assuming $70,400 to be the final amount, they earned $21,680 from the auction held in 1988.

It may seem unfair that Sachs could not get his painting when it was first located in 1988. The court case and FBI teletype provided no insight into who the couple was, or when or how they purchased *Russian School Children*. It was safe to assume that the auction house and legal advisors considered the couple "good faith" purchasers, a term used for a person who purchased property without knowing its previous history as stolen and protected in most state stolen property laws as the rightful owner. Even if the couple had complete knowledge of its hot history, it was nearly impossible to prove that in court. Too many years had passed before it resurfaced at the auction house.

The legal battles lasted almost six years and involved more than just ownership rights. There were countersuits for defamation of character and reimbursement of legal fees.[14] In the eyes of the court, Sachs willingly transferred a clear title in 1988 to the buyer. In the end, the judge granted ownership to the New York art dealer who sold *Russian School Children* to Spielberg in 1988 then exchanged a Rockwell painting of equal value in 2007.[15]

The FBI erroneously listed *Russian School Children* as an active stolen art case, which led to the lawsuit. The real loser, in this case, was perhaps Spielberg. He gave up a painting he legally owned, a title cleared a year before he purchased it from the New York art dealer in 1989.

Unfortunately, I could not share a photo of the painting with readers, as my small budget couldn't justify the hefty fee estimated for the license to reproduce it for the book. As of this writing, *Russian School Children* safely resided at The National Museum of American Illustration, located in Newport, Rhode Island. Readers can view it in person for a small admission price, but a quick internet search of the title provides a free peek at the controversial Rockwell. Readers will no longer find the painting in the NSAF database on the FBI website.

Maybe the FBI had the two St. Louis thefts backward since *Nude* was not on the NSAF database though still missing. Unfortunately, years of opportunities for someone to rediscover *Nude's* whereabouts also passed. Nevertheless, the false recovery of the Rockwell and the lawsuit that followed provided clues about the motive, the thief, and the movement of stolen art.

Russian School Children stayed within the States, moving from St. Louis to New Orleans (by the way, both were La Cosa Nostra crime cities in 1973). The couple likely purchased the painting in good faith and in the open market (i.e., art dealer, gallery, et cetera). A painting stolen in one city and moved to another was not typical of a petty thief.

Highly valued stolen art required a network capable of moving art from one city to the next, far enough away where an unsuspecting buyer might not recognize it as stolen art. The most obvious network between cities would have been through the organized crime Syndicate.

Understanding the movement of art stolen from a St. Louis gallery in 1973 and landing in a New Orleans auction in 1988 revealed new possibilities for *Nude* and its potential whereabouts.

THE ANATOMY OF A FENCING OPERATION

Three years after the Picasso and Rockwell paintings disappeared, the Associated Press reported stolen art ranking just behind illegal drug traffic in international crime. It was the earliest account I found where an investigator linked organized crime publicly to art theft stateside.

Around the same time, the DOJ released *Strategies for Combatting the Criminal Receiver of Stolen Goods*, a control manual for developing anti-fencing operations. Inside the document, a detailed profile described different types of fencing operations. Among them were profiles likely to target high-value goods, such as art, and differentiating the work of organized crime from stand-alone fencing operations.

The manual described the fence as someone who knowingly "receives, purchases, transports, conceals or possesses" stolen property.[16] The guideline established three types of fences, and I figured at least one of them could provide additional clues to the kind of operation behind the art thefts in St. Louis.

The least likely of the three was the "neighborhood fence." The neighborhood fence paid petty thieves for almost anything. This was not a specialty operation, nor the kind of operation to move highly valuable art pieces. The stolen merchandise was usually random victims of convenience like a lawnmower, a car, tools, car stereos, clothes, coins, and so on.

The second fencing operation was theft-for-order. It usually involved high-valued items and targeted a category of goods tied to the fence's specialty in business.

The manual described the "theft-for-order" fence as a businessman who operated a legal enterprise and moved stolen goods to a storefront operation. The storefront was just far enough away to elude local detection.

In this case, a storefront specializing in art and antiques received stolen art, just as an electronics store might receive hot stereo equipment. The operation lifted goods from one location and often sent them to another for reselling in a respectable storefront. They sold art mainly on the open market to good-faith buyers. Art that might have gone to the black market could remain with underworld figures.

The book exampled "short" distances as relocating stolen goods from one city to the outskirts of the same city. But this wouldn't preclude moving some stolen goods to other cities within reasonable distances. A central location like St. Louis might be perfect for an art fencing operation. St. Louis was ideally located with easy drives to Chicago, Kansas City, Little Rock, Memphis, Nashville, Indianapolis, Milwaukee, Minneapolis, Louisville, New Orleans, Detroit, and Cleveland. Most of them were also Syndicate cities in 1973.

Unscrupulous art dealers in those cities could fall into this type of fencing operation, making it a viable candidate for the missing Picasso. It also explains how the stolen Rockwell resurfaced in New Orleans. Keep in mind, those in pursuit of criminals wrote the anti-fencing manual, not the criminal fences. The rules the criminals played by might not be an exact fit for the textbook definition.

The third type of fence was the "set-up." The fence took a more active role in initiating and planning a theft. This was usually a fence interested in specialty goods. The "set-up" described how the fence gained information to plan the heist. It was typically through a relationship role targeting a small business or personal residence. The textbook definition, once again, might not be an exact match for planning a museum or gallery heist, but the basic principles could still apply.

In the case of stolen art from a museum, the "set-up" could also be an insider, like a security guard or a staff member no one would ever suspect, such as a quiet conservator. Of the multiple art thefts in St. Louis, *Nude* made the best case for having an insider because it happened during the daytime with security present.

However, a relationship was not always required for a "set-up" in a museum robbery. Art museums were public venues with valuables on display meant to be accessible to anyone. A fence was capable of estimating the value of art from other sources, such as recent auctions, criminal news reports, or catalog pricing.

A fence and/or thief could easily observe the art up close, monitor security for weaknesses, and watch security's response to hundreds of guests filing in and out of the building daily. The average visitor could converse with museum staff under ordinary circumstances without them knowing the person was collecting information for planning a heist.

The thief executed the fence's plan to retrieve what he wanted. According to the anti-fencing manual, to facilitate the "set-up," the fence often provided the vehicle to the thief. [17] Whoever walked into the art museum during business hours and walked out with *Nude* may have been a hired hand.

As a rule, fences remained safely in the background and did not participate in actually stealing. A thief caught stealing for a fencing operation usually had little impact on the fence's business. Even though the conspiracy law made it possible to convict a fence for just "conspiring" to steal and sell goods as part of a criminal racket, foreknowledge was challenging to prove. A fence could claim he did not know the goods were hot and avoid prosecution.

Most professional fences preferred to specialize in the goods they targeted. Art, for example, was the typical property of galleries, museums, and the upper class. Fences who targeted art brokered the theft for someone specifically or moved it to a storefront that specialized in art and antiques.

Art, like vending, was an unregulated industry. Transactions were completed with no government oversight. The inventory could be acquired illegally and sold without documenting the seller or buyer's name. If the Syndicate used local vending monopolies to control major sporting venue contracts across thirty states, then moving stolen art through criminally infiltrated storefronts in other cities was probably a walk in the park.

The DOJ generalized the type of "specialty" goods into two categories. Stereos and clothing were examples of high-volume/low-value goods and were the most frequently stolen and fenced items.

Hijacking a cargo of stereo equipment, for example, required a tightly controlled coordinated effort and carried larger risks. The fence had to invest in upfront costs to pull off the operation and, potentially, relabel products. Because the goods were low-value, the profit margin was much smaller, and the fence needed a continuous supply of stolen goods to make the racket profitable. The number of people and the frequency of thefts involved increased the risks that could ultimately lead to the fence's arrest and prosecution.

A professional fencing operation like this could operate independently, but in a city with organized crime, they benefited from a relationship with the Syndicate. The Mafia infiltration of transportation labor unions could have provided insight to distribution schedules and routes. Mafia members and associates could play the role of a tipster, providing insight on merchandise shipments for a fee.

The DOJ doubted that the Mafia would be interested in operating a fencing scheme that offered high risk and low profits like stereo merchandise. Instead, they might have allowed this type of operation to exist in its territory, as a "pay-to-play" offer the fence couldn't refuse.

The second category, low-volume/high-value items, provided higher profits and could be committed infrequently. Opting for a less risky theft operation, most fences preferred to target cars, jewelry, antiques, or eventually, art, but few could be successful. Pursuing art required more sophisticated knowledge of the market, specialized storefronts, or a line of criminal customers in the black market.

The DOJ considered "a sporadic" operation targeting high-valued items indicative of a Syndicate heist. But the federal government had not totally bridged the connection between organized crime and art as a currency on the black market, so most of the guidance focused on fencing in the open market.

The crackdown on LCN operations that began in 1971 in St. Louis could have motivated the Syndicate to turn to a safer scheme, using their professional fencing connections to take art. Missouri's weak stolen property laws and lack of security around art made it easy to steal, and it had a low risk of prosecution.

The unregulated art market was out of the government's watchful eye, like the storefronts that dealt with art and antiques. Fences could be informants and play on both sides of the law, which could be the perfect scenario for a new criminal scheme.

FENCING OPERATIONS IN ST. LOUIS

In 1976, the St. Louis police launched SCORE: Special Cover Operations for Resale Enforcement. Twelve undercover policemen operated a fencing operation out of a warehouse building. This was a neighborhood operation. In the end, they arrested seventy local criminals for fencing stolen goods over ten months.

The DOJ's anti-fencing guide considered this type of sting more harmful than helpful. It argued that it encouraged thefts and only caught petty thieves, not the fence that enabled the crime. The storefront sting illustrated local law enforcement's focus on "thieves" when the DOJ emphasized fences as the new target.

The DOJ also stated that neighborhood fences could operate in a city of professional fences or organized crime operations and never cross paths. SCORE would never catch the kind of fences targeting high-valued art.

One art theft ring emerged while investigating the history of St. Louis art thefts from the 1970s. Local authorities considered the thief, Ray Ellis*, a top-notch safe cracker. He wore multiple criminal hats as a thief and a fence capable of stealing high-valued goods and physically moving them across multiple states. Most fences stayed away from participating in the robberies, but I suppose Ellis's unique skills made him a unicorn among fences.

Law enforcement connected him to multiple local organized crime figures, primarily those allied with the faction that operated on the East Side of St. Louis. The Chicago OCSF team pursued him over a couple of years as a member of a fencing operation with direct ties to Syndicate figures.

The FBI arrested Ellis and his co-conspirators for stealing and moving goods across various states in 1977. The bust recovered stolen property from Mississippi, Wisconsin, Illinois, Missouri, and Florida. The thief rented some apartments in the St. Louis metro area as cold storage for the hot assets,[18] a term appropriately used as thieves waited for the investigative activity to subside. Once an investigation and media attention slowed, thieves moved the stolen goods to the next destination.

The Chicago strike force caught Ellis and his crew with about one hundred art objects. Additional storage locations uncovered more goods. The bust yielded about $1.3 million ($6.0 million in 2022) in stolen art, antiques, stained glass, jade, jewelry, furs, and other valuables. The sheer volume of goods was quite impressive.

Ellis also had close ties to the East Side faction, historically known as an arm of the Chicago Outfit.[19] Either the fencing operation took orders from the Chicago Mafia or the criminal investigation defaulted to the Chicago OCSF after the St. Louis unit disbanded in 1976.

His arrest busted a myth that art needed a buyer in the wings, a comment cited in the case of the stolen Picasso. Thieves were capable of stashing stolen art with other valuables. This provided flexibility for the scheme. The operation could sell art to a shady dealer, an obsessive art enthusiast, a storefront, or head for the black market. The outcome could place art in any city, state, or country.

Ellis's operation focused on a variety of high-value items. He and his crew committed multistate residential robberies, stealing art from private collections. Not one report indicated the art came from a gallery or museum. Personal art collections found in homes made up the majority of art thefts in the United States, and museums made up the least.

A year before the federal bust, local police caught Ellis and another hoodlum during a one-weekend binge of thefts in West County. Ellis was out on bond when he was arrested for selling stolen glass artworks to the undercover federal agent.

He boasted to the federal operatives that he had friends in law enforcement who warned him to stay away from the St. Louis police operation, SCORE. He bragged about having sold stolen goods to friends in the force, adding fuel to the fire. He told agents that the White fences were tipped off, explaining why most arrests were of Blacks.[20]

After his arrest, Ellis's claims hit the press. The police department denied any leaks in operation SCORE and responded that the suspect only knew of SCORE from recent news reports. They believed he used the story to "impress" the undercover federal agents posing as buyers.[21]

This was police speculation meant to protect department credibility. Any claim of potential corruption allowed to fester in the news would have been bad publicity for the city. For the Syndicate to thrive in any market, corruption must exist in law enforcement. When it happened, it was not supposed to be obvious; otherwise, it would not be effective. Department corruption existed in prior decades, and the '70s was likely no different.

The OCSF sting put a significant dent into the fencing operation's stolen assets when they recovered over a million dollars in stolen goods. Ellis attempted to sell lifted glass artworks to an undercover FBI agent, a tactic agents deployed to break up fencing schemes.[22]

Ellis turned himself over to federal authorities in January of 1978 after a grand jury indicted him and others on the conspiracy and transportation of stolen property. By March, he faced racketeering charges as a member of the multistate fencing operation.

The anti-fencing strategies made a distinct point that the goal of any anti-fencing unit was to catch and prosecute the fence, a 180-degree turn from prior years. The fence enabled thieves to plan crimes and move stolen goods to buyers or markets. The DOJ said chasing thieves and Syndicate figures connected to a fencing operation were distractions for an anti-fencing unit. Arresting a fence cut off income to thieves and disrupted the flow of stolen goods, resulting in a negative impact to the entire channel.

However, in 1973, that was not the strategy. Fences were seen as low-level criminals and an unimportant cog in a fencing operation. Fences were used to catch thieves or gain insight into organized crime operations. Therefore, the FBI used fences as criminal informants.

A criminal informant was someone who became an informant to avoid jail time, but also could be labeled as a snitch in the underworld, if not careful. Fences became pretty versed in balancing the two roles. Being a criminal informant in 1973 was practically an art.

When a fence became an FBI informant, they were assigned a handler. The handler collected information, filing typed reports with the informant's file and anyone the information might pertain to. Despite the purge of local art theft records, one relative informant report remained about stolen art in St. Louis.

The five-page criminal informant report provided new insight into fencing art specific to 1973. Yet there was one strange caveat to the memo. I found it in a government archive under the JFK assassination files released in 2017—not the typical location one would expect to find an informant report on stolen art. However, this memo had historical value, which kept it from the teeth of an FBI shredder over the past five decades.

8

The Art of the Informant

THE ROLE OF THE INFORMANT became a critical tool for developing inside information on all organized crime, which included Syndicate activity and fencing operations. The problem in 1973 was the police and FBI made criminal informants out of fences. They wrongly perceived fences as simply low-level players in stolen property crimes. Fences usually planned, organized, executed, and moved stolen goods. They were specialists in their field, highly intelligent, sometimes charming, and always scheming. They could also be violent and dangerous.

Investigative agencies used three types of informants: 1) law enforcement, 2) the ordinary citizen, and 3) the criminal informant. The criminal informant held the most value in the case of the St. Louis art crimes.

The problem with turning a criminal into an informant was the reliability of the information. A criminal could lie and cheat to get what they wanted or prevent others from jeopardizing their world of crime, and a fence or an art thief was no exception to that rule. Essentially, they could manipulate the informant's role to their advantage. Therefore, the information they provided came with a potential land mine of problems.

To help alleviate the problem posed by informants, judges used the Aguilar test, according to a 1976 DOJ manual on strategies for combatting fences. This was a two-prong test to determine reliability of the informant and information. The first part of the test required the law enforcement officer to describe the underlying circumstances from which a judge could determine that the informant was a reliable source. The second part of the test required the officer to describe the underlying circumstances from which the judge could determine that the informant's information was reliable and not the result of mere suspicion. Both prongs of this test must be satisfied before probable cause can be established, a requirement for an arrest or search warrant.[1]

Regarding the criminal informant, passing the test of reliability was threefold. The operative word was "reliable" since the criminal informant posed a different problem than the other two types. Basically, a criminal was interested in avoiding a prison sentence of his own while not getting labeled a snitch by his criminal associates.

If the criminal informant provided accurate information in the past that led to arrests, recovery of stolen property, convictions, or other helpful information to law enforcement, they passed the first test. If the informant made admissions or turned over evidence against his own "penal interests," they met the second requirement of reliability. The third condition considered the length of time the criminal served in their role as an informant.[2]

Firsthand information was preferred to hearsay, and it had to be timely to the request for a search warrant. Stolen goods moved quickly in a professional fencing operation, and information on the whereabouts of the property expired quickly.

The role required secrecy to protect the informant from retaliation from criminal associates. If a fence or thief chose to be a criminal informant, they faced a new risk from their criminal associates. If labeled a snitch, they faced certain dangers, including death.

A criminal arrested, released, and never prosecuted drew suspicion among associates. Sometimes the agency used cover stories to protect the informant and prevent them from being harmed. The cover story also allowed the fence to slip back into their criminal role to maintain contacts and gather intelligence for the FBI or police. The agent assigned to an informant was the "handler." The handler discreetly met with the informant, collected insight on potential leads in a crime, and reported information without compromising the source's identity.

Informants threatened the criminal organization. Yet criminals who hated snitches eventually became snitches too. It seemed to be the trend from the so-called lowly fence to the highest ranks of organized crime.

Given the inherent risk of being a snitch, a short jail sentence seemed more attractive than being shot, stuffed in a trunk, then rolled into the Mississippi as catfish bait. Despite the threat, some criminals chose to become informants to avoid incarceration.

One expert criminal psychologist and researcher interviewed hundreds of offenders, diving into their childhoods to better understand their earliest career aspirations. Criminals frequently mentioned their youthful desire to become police officers.[3]

It was an interesting observation. Lawbreakers may have held a deep desire to help solve crimes, and becoming an informant let them play on both sides of the law. Maybe it also explained why corrupt officers hid behind badges, or brave officers masqueraded as hoodlums. Moreover, it explained why law enforcement agencies successfully developed informants out of crooks.[4]

Fences offered law enforcement store discounts, adding to their image of being harmless, minor players, perhaps even victims of receiving stolen property in error. The truth was that the fence gave a reason for the thief to steal. As long as fences existed, others were willing to steal and cash in whatever goods the fence needed. Fences made career thieves.

A thief and a fence both benefited from their relationship. The fence used a skilled thief to successfully steal property and reduce their own exposure. In return, the thief earned quick cash without having to find a buyer for the stolen goods. Having a source to quickly hand off the property reduced a thief's own risk of arrest.

Because stolen property convictions were difficult, and sentences for stolen art often light, fencing art became an attractive, profitable, criminal strategy with minimal risks.

WHEN A FENCE BECOMES AN INFORMANT

One Saturday in early September 1972, two white males dressed in business suits, one of them with an attaché case, arrived at a Central West End jewelry store just after hours. Believing them to be prospective customers, the owner's fourteen-year-old son unlocked the door and let them in for business. The men were there to rob the store. One thief took his pistol and struck the boy's mother to the floor. They tied each victim to a chair as they ransacked the store. The two robbers made off with $250,000 worth of jewelry, including the woman's wedding rings.[5]

The police arrested and released their first suspect on bond a month after the robbery. He was a twenty-seven-year-old from the Missouri boot heel. Soon after, his associates lured him to Little Rock, Arkansas, where he was shot and killed. Police arrested a second suspect, age thirty-seven, for the jewelry robbery and the suspected killing of his accomplice. After he was released on bond, he went to Arkansas, where police shot the suspect numerous times as he left a Little Rock drugstore after allegedly robbing it. The two Missouri men who had pulled off the St. Louis jewelry heist in early September were dead by early November.[6]

The FBI and local police had suspected others to be involved in the heist, potentially a more extensive operation than just the two thieves. Before mid-November, police arrested an accomplice, James Kelly*.[7] Kelly dealt in art and antiques and ran a shop next door to the heist scene. The paper described Kelly as a friend of the store owners robbed of their jewels. Investigators alleged Kelly used his friendship to gain inside information then provided it to robbers to execute the heist. It was a textbook "set-up" robbery scheme.

The court released Kelly on bond. His name disappeared from news coverage, indicating that the prosecutor's office dropped the charges against him. Kelly was never mentioned again as part of the case and became an FBI informant. This was a relevant example of how fences (and other criminals) avoided prosecution.

A couple of months passed after Kelly's arrest when Neal Jurgen* was indicted for transporting the stolen jewelry across the state line from Missouri to Arkansas. Jurgen, a St. Louis restaurant proprietor, faced the heat for a crime planned, organized, and committed by multiple associates. But he stood alone on trial in the summer of 1973. Fortunately for the lone defendant, he had an experienced criminal lawyer, Monte Randolph*.

Randolph had a well-rounded legal background as a prosecuting attorney and a criminal defense lawyer. He had been in private practice for about four years when he took on the case of the Maryland Plaza jewelry heist. Randolph had been involved in high-profile cases working for the criminal law firm of Morris Shenker in the 1960s. During his stint with Shenker, he represented a few notable St. Louis hoodlums. Perhaps his most sensational case occurred in 1962 when Randolph successfully defended a woman accused of putting a contract hit on her husband, a local realtor.

But ten years had passed, and Randolph was in private practice defending the local man accused of taking stolen jewelry across the state line, a federal offense. He faced what seemed to be a tight case against his client.

A relative of one of the dead thieves took the witness stand for the prosecution. He testified that Jurgen arrived at his Wentzville home with a small suitcase containing the stolen gems just hours after the holdup to keep the loot safe. Several hours later, the two thieves and the defendant returned with a fourth man who examined at least part of the loot.

The prosecution called their next witness to further implicate Jurgen in the heist. The witness pointed to Jurgen as one of the men who convinced him the jewelry for sale was not hot. He brought Jurgen and the "estate" jewelry to his boss, the hotel owner.

The hotel owner, a third witness in the case, took the stand, stating he purchased fifty-one pieces of jewelry from the defendant just five days after the robbery. He said Jurgen had represented himself as the person who inherited the jewels and was in a hurry to sell them to pay the estate taxes.[8]

When Jurgen took the stand in the jewelry heist case, he testified he did not know the goods were hot. The two robbers, he claimed, were frequent patrons at his restaurant and business associates in the kitchen restoration business, buying and selling used equipment. He testified he sold the jewelry as a favor, believing the men needed the cash to pay off estate taxes.

Randolph argued his client's travels with the thieves were purely for business and that Jurgen received no money in return, thus lacking a motive for the crime.[9]

Deliberation took just five hours. The case against the prime suspect was that he transported stolen goods across the state line, a federal offense. At first, the jury overwhelmingly voted in favor of conviction until one juror convincingly argued that the government only proved the defendant to be a lousy judge of character. He allegedly convinced the rest of the jurors that the government failed to prove the defendant was involved in transporting stolen property to Arkansas. The jury flipped their initial vote and acquitted Jurgen.[10]

Soon after the trial ended, news broke of possible jury tampering. The influential juror and the defendant were associated with the same (Mafia-compromised) labor union, drawing further suspicion. Randolph immediately called for an investigation, claiming it was critical to maintaining the lawyers' and court system's integrity and reputation. The tampering investigation yielded no charges other than the decision to release the accused juror from further jury duty (hardly a punishment if you have ever served on one). Without evidence, the issue died in the hands of federal prosecutors.[11]

Jurgen won his case in June 1973, partially due to Randolph's astute defense, the persuasion of one juror, and maybe even the help of this uncle, a Kansas City–area judge. The judge was seen slipping notes to Randolph during the trial.

The Kansas City judge was a former lawyer, aiding his nephew during the trial. As a former lawyer, he could no longer practice law once he became a judge. He sat close enough to pass notes to Randolph but far away enough to pass as legal. The uncle also interrogated witnesses after the FBI investigators interviewed them. Uncle Judge argued he never crossed the line and helped his family, as anyone would do in his position. The Missouri Commission on Retirement, Removal, and Discipline investigated and rendered him innocent of any misconduct.[12]

The case of the jewelry heist had its twists and turns. The federal judge presiding over the trial was William Webster. Five years after the case, Webster became just the third director of the FBI in its fifty-plus-year history. Randolph left his private practice to become a St. Louis circuit judge in 1975. Jurgen was sighted playing golf with local Mafia characters. At the same time, his new attorney argued double jeopardy in court to prevent a new trial over the stolen jewelry in

Arkansas. And Kelly, the accomplice named in the heist, would skirt prosecution and become an FBI criminal informant.

The jewelry heist case connected organized crime to high-valued property thefts. It demonstrated the ability to move stolen goods across a Syndicated network to other states and cities. When Kelly became a criminal informant, the federal government was interested in a strategy to gain inside information on organized crime to cripple Mafia operations, not recover stolen property. Instead, Kelly's stint as an FBI informant would be the catalyst behind a bureau memo that would also have Webster and Randolph crossing paths again, but this time on a national stage involving assassination conspiracies.

THE BIRTH OF AN INFORMANT

Around August 1973, about two months after the trial ended, Kelly quietly opened a new art and antique store just a block from the site of the jewelry robbery on Maryland Avenue.

Perhaps the government could not prove its case against Kelly and dropped the charges. Maybe he gave them something they wanted all along: information on others involved in the robbery. Law enforcement told the local newspaper that the state's chief witness against Kelly refused to testify in this case.[13] I suspected the FBI planted the story as a cover to protect Kelly's new identity as an FBI informant, a role he started in 1973 in exchange for his freedom.

As another precaution, the FBI replaced each informant name with a number to protect their real identity, even from other agents who could access the files. Kelly's number included SL (St. Louis), four random digits, and the letters P-C-I. The code "PCI" provided insight into his status when his handler wrote the report in early 1974. PCI meant potential criminal informant or potential confidential informant. The title of criminal or confidential informant reflected the leniency in a case against him in exchange for information.

"Potential" indicated the FBI had not established Kelly as a reliable source. It was a process that might take some time and additional proof to confirm his information was reliable.

Rather than face jail time for his role in the robbery, it would have been in his best interest to agree to become an informant for the bureau. No one knew what information he provided to gain leniency, but it came with the expectation of providing information on other crimes. Kelly had a reputation as a fence. Because fences were considered low-level players in a criminal scheme, law enforcement used fences as informants, usually to catch thieves or gather intelligence on bigger targets connected to organized crime. In this case, the FBI could use the informant to capture either type of criminal; historically, the information points to their interest in organized crime activities.

The following references content from the FBI informant report. The original FBI report arranged the content following the timeline of Kelly's conversation with a suspected art thief. Kelly met the suspect around August of 1973 and reported conversations he had with the suspect through January of 1974. The FBI's subject of the informant was valuable artifacts stolen from the Jefferson Memorial at Forest Park.

I organized the information by the type of discussions during those eight months. First, explaining the local art thefts relevant to chasing answers behind the motive for stealing *Nude* and predicting its likely whereabouts.

Then I included information that highlighted the alleged violence. It included acts that ultimately led the government to preserve the memo in the JFK assassination files.

THE CRIMINAL INFORMANT AND THE ART THIEF

The National Archives and Records Administration (NARA) recently released one complete FBI memorandum involving stolen art. On March 13, 1974, an FBI agent, assumed to be the handler, met Kelly, the criminal informant, near Manchester and Choteau Avenues in south St. Louis. The contents of the meeting, recorded in a memo dated a few days later, were available to the public for several years, but only recently were they released with no redactions. Multiple references about stolen art between 1973 and 1974 were included, making them relative to the time *Nude* disappeared from the art museum.

The memo's subject was the theft of two silver portrait busts, one of the famous aviator Charles Lindbergh and the other of his wife, Anne Morrow Lindbergh. Thieves stole them from the Missouri History Museum in early January 1974. The history museum, erected in 1913 and also located in Forest Park, looked slightly different than it does today. In 1974, only the pillars of the history museum enclosed the seated president, Thomas Jefferson. Back then, locals knew the building as the Jefferson Memorial.

A sunken courtyard, built in 1970 and now enclosed, once provided visitors direct access to a lower level of the museum. The green space featured an elegant staircase leading to the museum's lower level. The central area was surrounded by flattering arches that hid the glass windows and doors that were locked after hours, a perfect venue for the thieves who pulled off a night-time smash-and-grab robbery.[14]

When the story of the robbery broke in the news, each figure was valued at $25,000. Along with the statues, the local paper reported "a 10-inch gold cup commemorating Lindbergh's historic flight across the Atlantic in 1927."[15] Sources valued the cup at just $500 when it went missing. The cup was returned within a week of the robbery. Perhaps the cup's low value made it harder to sell or the thief was sentimental about the historical significance of the Lindbergh flight and decided to return it to the museum. An anonymous tip led St. Louis County police to the entrance of a training school for troubled boys, where they found the cup. The thief selected this location to shift suspicion to juvenile inmates of the North County school.

The silver statues, just eighteen inches tall, were considerably more valuable than the gold cup. Shinzo Fukuhara, a Japanese artist known for his exceptional photography, presented the sculptures to the couple in August 1931. The inscription on the busts read, "To Col. Charles A. Lindbergh and Mrs. Anne Morrow Lindbergh, best wishes and sincere congratulations, Washington–Tokyo flight." Lindbergh donated the collection to the Jefferson Memorial in 1932.

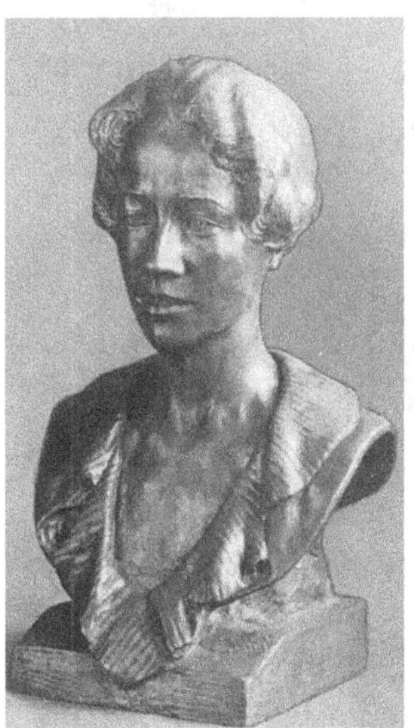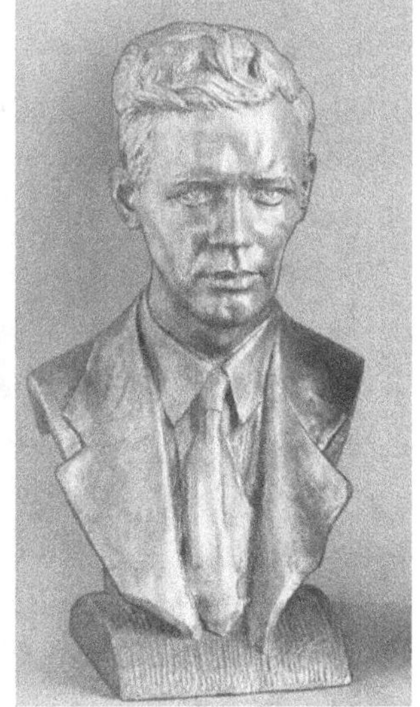

The missing Charles and Anne Lindbergh Busts (1932)
By Shinzo Fukuhara
The silver busts are 18 inches tall,
each inscribed with congratulatory words, including
"Washington–Tokio [Tokyo] flight, August 1931."

Aside from selling collectibles, art, and antiques, Kelly also restored art. His legitimate storefront business dealt in antiques and fine paintings. The kind of goods taken from the history museum made Kelly an ideal fence for thieves looking to cash in on the goods or maybe even assess the value of their score. He also knew enough to understand the risks of acquiring hot art, especially as an informant under the watchful eye of the FBI.

In March 1974, Kelly met his handler in south St. Louis City. More than a year had passed since federal prosecutors dropped the charges against him in the jewelry heist. Kelly had a lot of material to share with his handler but absolutely no intention of testifying to it if ever asked.[16]

The 1974 informant memorandum summarized eight months of interactions between Kelly and a suspected art thief. The informant provided details of conversations he had directly with a man he claimed to have only met in August 1973, Robert Meier*.

FBI wiretaps had the advantage of recording the exact conversation between two or more people. The informant report, however, was a one-sided recall of conversations. Kelly's report was a debriefing of conversations he had with Meier, told to his handler months after they occurred.

According to Kelly, Meier shared his intentions to steal from the Jefferson Memorial and even asked Kelly if he had any interest in pieces from the history museum. Kelly explained his most recent troubles with the law and advised that any goods from the museum would be too hot to handle. Kelly declined the offer to participate.

Meier counterproposed a different use for stolen artifacts. He suggested taking the "commemorative pieces" to "set up his enemies" by "stashing them in the trunk of somebody's car."

A few days after the conversation, Kelly said he had heard about the Jefferson Memorial robbery. The burglary happened on January 4, 1974. In a matter of days, Kelly reported, Meier came to his antique store. Though he did not speak of the robbery, Kelly described him as uncharacteristically disheveled and unshaven. He said Meier proclaimed he "had his hands full."[17] Kelly told the agent this was the last time he interacted with the suspect.

Perhaps it was the heat from the robbery that frazzled Meier, or maybe a combination of issues. At about the same time, he was a defendant in a civil case. The plaintiff sought reimbursement for the value of several vending machines that went missing under his care.[18] The two silver Lindbergh statues, valued at $50,000 combined, provided enough money to potentially cover the damages in the civil lawsuit he faced—maybe even the motive for the robbery.

Meier shared quite a bit of his life story with Kelly over those eight months, and Kelly told plenty of it to his FBI handler. Kelly reported other conversations about potential heists. He explained that Meier was interested in hitting the Hollander Gallery.[19]

The Hollander, a private gallery in north St. Louis County, prepared for an extensive exhibit in late 1973. It featured several oils, watercolors, and drawings by notable artists. Among the collection were works of famous painters: Monet, Kandinsky, Renoir, O'Keeffe, and Remington. A full-page feature story on the gallery, its owners, and its valuables from the collection appeared in the local newspaper in December 1973.

Criminals read the news; advertised exhibits were business leads for the next score. If the story included values, that was a bonus because an art thief could use the retail value to negotiate with a potential buyer.

The Hollander brothers were avid collectors of paintings, jade, and African art. They displayed their vast treasures in the most unlikely place: a Zenith television showroom, which doubled as an art gallery. In July of 1973, the Hollander brothers acquired a focal piece, a painting by Auguste Renoir, another famous French artist. They paid $200,000—information shared in the news—unknowingly bragging to every potential art thief reading the feature story.

The Hollander Gallery would have been a much larger score than the history museum. Perhaps the untimely decision to rob the Jefferson Memorial and a pending civil case put the Hollander scheme on the back burner. The Hollander's collection remained safe.

A ROCKWELL PAINTING ON THE MOVE

As mentioned in the previous chapter, a private investigator looked into the theft of *Russian School Children* in 1973. After finding who had it, he recommended leaving it alone, stating the criminals were dangerous and would likely steal it back even if he recovered it. The crime was committed two months after someone removed *Nude* from the art museum.

Kelly provided insight into what clearly seemed to be the stolen Rockwell painting from the gallery in St. Louis. The Clayton gallery that once displayed *Russian School Children* was located on the same street as Kelly's store; the two places were only a couple of miles apart. According to Kelly, Meier said he had a Norman Rockwell painting recently stolen.[20]

The FBI report did not explicitly name *Russian School Children*. However, Meier presented a Rockwell to Kelly around August, after it was stolen in June. The crime was a smash-and-grab robbery, the same type used to rob the history museum.

It had to be the Rockwell stolen from the gallery that resurfaced in New Orleans in 1988. Meier told Kelly he intended "to have it on ice" but was willing to sell it to him for just $5,000. Kelly considered the purchase but claimed to have contacted his lawyer first to see if he could sell it back to the insurance company.

Kelly made a curious move for someone who, on the one hand, showed concern about handling the hot museum items. On the other hand, he thought it was okay to buy a hot painting to collect money from the insurance company for its return.

According to Kelly, the insurance company told his lawyer they were not interested in paying for it. Meier returned to the shop a few days later with a better offer, and the final price dropped as low as $2,000. With no deal, the suspect claimed it was destined for "cold storage." This was the last time the informant claimed to have heard of the Rockwell painting.

If the informant's timing was accurate, the offer came just two months after thieves took *Russian School Children* from the Clayton gallery. The insurance company could have possibly recovered *Russian School Children* in 1973 through Kelly. This assumes Kelly's lawyer actually contacted the insurance company. The attorney may have told Kelly a white lie to keep him out of trouble.

Meier declared to Kelly, "if there was anything in St. Louis that he wanted to buy, he would have it stolen and sell it to him at the right price."[21] Meier never said *he* stole the painting but *had* it stolen, implying he worked with others and did not participate directly in the *physical* theft.

The description matched the role of a broker fence. A broker fence was independent, focused on planning and executing heists, and did not own a storefront. Meier obviously did not have a store since he was engaging Kelly for this service. A local broker fence could be an associate of an organized crime ring capable of fencing stolen property from their local city and moving into an affiliate city in their criminal network.

Kelly believed that Meier still had the Lindbergh statues and the Rockwell in his possession, advising the agent of the items' general whereabouts. Nevertheless, months had elapsed between Kelly's interaction with Meier and reporting the information to the FBI. Kelly's status as a new informant was possibly another problem. Without hard evidence and a reliable informant, no judge would grant a warrant to search the suspect's property.

As excited as I was to finally see information about the Rockwell painting, I was disappointed to find nothing on the missing Picasso. I can't help but wonder if the Picasso sat in cold storage with *Russian School Children* in St. Louis. If the thief had it, would he have offered it to Kelly? Did he hold on to it? Maybe *Nude* moved to another city like the Rockwell, or perhaps another thief took the Picasso from the art museum.

The chance to speculate on what may have happened was only made possible because of the other information found inside this FBI report. If the memo was just about stolen art, the document would have been purged like the rest of the art case files.

SWORDLESS FENCING STILL DANGEROUS

Kelly was no angel. A jewelry robbery got him in this predicament as a federal informer and now he retold another criminal's secrets—secrets Kelly was unwilling to repeat if asked to testify. Similarly, Meier told Kelly he would never talk to the police, no matter the circumstances. The two criminals had a lot in common: the ability to keep quiet when it mattered and a desire for fencing art.

The newly recruited FBI informant painted Meier as a criminal always scheming for his next score. It was a textbook description of a criminal mind and no different than a criminal informant.

The police and FBI knew Kelly was a fence and suspected his store was a legal front used to sell stolen art, antiques, and other collectibles. It was likely why the FBI met Kelly after the Lindbergh silver busts disappeared and why Meier became friendly with Kelly.

Kelly described Meier as intelligent and said he was very knowledgeable about antiques. Meier's "long Hoover sheet" only indicated he was a former car thief with no criminal acts of violence. After his career as a car thief, he moved on to the vending equipment business, a Mafia monopoly in St. Louis. Meier raised the score and lowered the risk when he set his sight on stealing art and antiques.

Kelly's description painted Meier as a dangerous man with a propensity for violence. It was either something Kelly wanted the FBI to believe or a true statement about the suspect. Violence, after all, was typically how organized criminals disciplined each other if betrayed.

Kelly opened his new store near Maryland Plaza shortly before meeting Meier for the first time. He was unloading boxes when he recalled an encounter with a young, professional-looking couple that entered the store. He compared their appearance to "an affluent doctor and his wife."[22]

The couple inquired about a broken piece of porcelain, wanting to know if it were Dresden or Meissen. The informant confirmed the piece as Dresden and explained it was for sale for ten dollars. The Meissen factory has made porcelain products in Dresden, Germany, since the early 1700s. A piece from a collection, especially if old, would be pretty valuable, but this was a small, broken item worth very little. The couple finished browsing, bought nothing, and left the shop.

The FBI agent described Meier as a middle-aged, stocky man who typically wore a sports jacket, tie, and black horn-rimmed glasses. The agent said he gave the "appearance of a successful jewelry businessman."[23]

The first time Meier entered Kelly's store in August 1973, he had suspicions about the informant. He wondered if the jewelry heist accomplice was a snitch, just as the FBI wondered if Kelly was a reliable informant.

Meier visited the store more than once before giving Kelly his name. It took multiple visits before Meier introduced himself to the informant. And when he did, he name-dropped the lawyer, Monte Randolph, in the introduction. He claimed to be both a client and a friend of Randolph. Meier knew Kelly would recognize the lawyer's name. Less than two months had passed since Randolph successfully defended the main suspect in the jewelry heist, the same heist that changed Kelly's status to FBI informant.

Meier likely wondered if Kelly ratted on the man acquitted in the heist weeks earlier. Kelly's name had been in the newspaper for his role in the jewelry robbery, and his disappearance from the case was not a secret. Meier definitely knew Randolph and may have used this to get a reaction from Kelly. Meier also had to know Kelly's role as a fence. No one just walked into a store assuming a shop owner was a fence.

Kelly described the conversations as businesslike. According to the FBI memo, the two suspected fences mainly talked about collectibles, some of which the man brought to the shop for the informant to estimate the retail value.

Meier's first interactions with Kelly tested his knowledge and trustworthiness as a potential outlet for his stolen goods. Soon the conversation turned dark. Meier explained to Kelly that he sent the young couple to his store to case the shop. He intended for them to return to the store and "knock him off," referring to Kelly, but then called off the hit, believing Kelly was not a snitch and could be trusted.[24]

Months later, Kelly described another incident that portrayed Meier as dangerous. He told the agent that the suspect informed him of his plans to take out a snitch then called him after the deed was completed. The next day, the informant read about a killing in north St. Louis, believing the murdered man may have been the target. Meier may have told Kelly about his plans to take out a snitch as a scare tactic. Crime in north St. Louis was not new, and the slaying Kelly read of in the newspaper could have been coincidental.[25]

The FBI agent did not expand on the alleged murder. It would have been a St. Louis city police case to solve. A handwritten comment on the memo's first page that stated, "Notify locals of info re killing," would eventually need clarification.

In the fall of 1973, Meier and Kelly met for dinner. Kelly reported this was at Meier's request. Afterward, the two headed back to Kelly's place for a couple of drinks. It was there Meier dropped the bombshell: two men offered him money to kill Martin Luther King, Jr., the famous civil rights leader gunned down five years earlier.

King died in front of the Lorraine Motel in Memphis, Tennessee, on April 15, 1968. Meier told the tale to Kelly while King's killer, James Earl Ray, rotted in a Tennessee prison for the crime. Ray pleaded guilty to the assassination and forfeited a trial in March 10, 1969. He tried to change his plea three days later, a request he subsequently repeated and always denied.

Kelly regurgitated Meier's story of the offer to the FBI agent. This became part of the FBI memorandum, ultimately securing the document as historical evidence.

The FBI memo was written when national news outlets shared stories of Ray begging the courts to give him a chance to change his plea to not guilty and face trial. Ray also had a direct connection to St. Louis. He grew up in the metro area, and two of his siblings lived in the city and ran a South City bar when Ray escaped from the Missouri State Penitentiary. He began serving a twenty-year jail sentence in 1959 for robbing a St. Louis Kroger grocery store.

Despite Meier's claim and Ray's connection to St. Louis, the agent didn't write this part of the memo with any more importance than the rest of the report. It was located in the middle of the report and consisted of just one, seven-sentence paragraph. The story was not in bold, separately flagged for attention, nor reported to any of the other FBI offices in charge of the King murder case.

The claim didn't move the FBI agent into action, perhaps because the agent viewed the case as closed. King had daily threats on his life in the 1960s, and maybe the agent considered Meier's tale to be one more quack claim.

The FBI agent ended the memo with some facts about Meier. The suspect was believed to be engaged in contacting customers for a vending business. In addition, Meier was married to the sister of ex-con J.P. Spacanelli*.

The memo also did not include the fact that Spacanelli was the middleman hired by the dead realtor's wife to arrange the killing.

Shenker's firm represented Spacanelli and the victim's wife in separate trials. Randolph was the lawyer who convinced a jury the wife was innocent. If counting, this was the third potential "contract" killing referred to in the memo.

Spacanelli served his sentence at the Missouri State Penitentiary simultaneously with Ray. Spacanelli was sentenced to life in prison in 1963 but was paroled in 1973. The two prison inmates were housed in the same cell block when Ray escaped in 1967.

Even so, the FBI agent treated Meier's statement to Kelly as unimportant. Then he spelled Meier's name wrong and inadvertently created a second file on the suspect in the art thefts. Over the next couple of years, FBI agents would continue to overlook Meier's *other* file. The bones of a conspiracy to kill King were there, but the FBI memorandum remained dormant for four years because of a simple mistake.

After getting over the surprise of a St. Louis plot to kill a highly regarded historical figure, I came to appreciate the remaining guts of the memo. I suppose anyone who didn't know about the St. Louis art thefts would completely ignore those parts of the document. But to understand the motive behind the disappearance of *Nude*, the FBI memo offered insight into the local world of art theft.

Kelly was a fence with a storefront. Meier was a broker fence, apparently with a robbery crew. Each had a penchant for high-value targets like art. They favored the art found in museums and galleries, whereas Ellis and his crew preferred robbing residential properties.

The public didn't know where the Picasso or Rockwell paintings disappeared to in 1973. Only in recent years did information about *Russian School Children* resurface in a lawsuit triggered by an FBI database error.

The changes in strategy to catch a fence would yield a victory for the investigators in the 1978 museum thefts and further support the theory that organized crime most likely ordered the theft of *Nude*.

The Art of Theft & Conspiracy

THE 1973 AND 1978 ROBBERIES both took place in the east wing of the Saint Louis Art Museum. The heists were drastically different, which might reflect unrelated thefts. Then again, two distinctly altered environments existed in the museum's east wing in those two years. If so, *Nude* may have been the first of a string of thefts that all had potential ties to organized crime.

By the early 1970s, the City Art Museum of St. Louis gave off an ominous vibe as it perched atop Art Hill like a gray fortress. The east and west wings flanked the museum entrance with an all-concrete façade. The walls were dingy and appeared impenetrable. To say it was uninviting was an understatement.

When St. Louisans agreed to a new sales tax in 1972 to fund the City Art Museum of St. Louis, there was a renewed hope to save the museum for future generations. It required a drastic makeover, but its budget was far below the funds needed to protect the collection.

In 1973, the quiet daytime theft of the Picasso might have been a wake-up call for the city and the museum. At that very moment, the art epidemic arrived at its doorstep. The museum added thefts to a growing list of threats the art collection faced. The others included indoor pollution, inadequate staffing, humidity, and lack of space. Security had to be a priority, just as it was for most art museums.

The art museum began planning strategies for raising funds necessary to support the renovations and address the problems. By 1974, the museum hired an architectural firm from New York to tackle its many issues, including security. The first renovation phase began in 1975. This phase focused on restoring the museum to its original design and expanding the gallery space.[1] The museum's east wing closed for renovation, and the museum's name soon changed to the Saint Louis Art Museum, both signs of the good to come.

The building's concrete walls were cleaned, and a fifteen-foot-tall window was added to each façade of the east and west wings. The top-curved window, double-pane glass, and trim color complemented the main gallery windows located on the main entrance's upper roof. The renovation architects designed the window frames to fit into the arched, decorative alcoves, which were previously filled with stone blocks. The blocks were once the backdrop for a large pedestal that occasionally held a statue.

The windows seemed to have added new life to the museum, giving it the appearance of having eyes to gaze upon the beauty of Forest Park. In return, park-goers felt welcomed to explore the beauty inside. The invitation was to all, and those with ill intent could not resist its new charm.

Critics of the renovation plan may have objected to the numerous changes or the price, but those feelings changed once they entered the private grand reopening on December 1, 1977. The renovated Saint Louis Art Museum exposed a beautiful space, restored to the original intent of its architect Cass Gilbert.

The tall cubicle of Gallery 16, where *Nude* once hung, was finally removed. Once again, visitors had an unobstructed view of the east and west wings as they stood at the center of Sculpture Hall, just as Gilbert intended. Guests moved freely from room to room and reached an exit or a stairway without the aid of a staff member. The beautiful, leak-free skylights returned natural light into the galleries below, yet they were carefully designed to protect the art from harmful sunrays. Gilbert would have looked at the museum restoration project with great delight.

The museum renumbered the second-floor galleries, and Gallery 16 became Gallery 216. The "two" represented the museum's second floor. The basement that once held administrative offices became floor one of the new gallery space. The museum displayed most of its collection for the first time in decades. Art pieces were no longer at risk of environmental damage from indoor pollution or the humid St. Louis summers. The open space would not hide a daytime thief behind an obscure wall as it did five years prior.

The architects armed the museum with a new alarm system, although this was not something they had announced publicly. It was not just any system but one of the most sophisticated security systems available in 1977.

When the museum opened on December 1, it was well-equipped to detect motion in its galleries and forbidden entry. All access points at the ground level would notify security if someone attempted to enter after visiting hours. No one would drop down from the newly fixed skylights without setting off the motion detector. A museum architect on the multimillion-dollar project said, "Any penetration of the museum by anything larger than a rat—even by tunneling from below—will trigger it."[2] His words were entirely accurate.

Art thieves kept their distance from Art Hill during the art museum's two-and-a-half-year restoration. On multiple occasions between 1974 and 1977, crooks stole from the Jefferson Memorial and Arts

International Gallery in Clayton. The same gallery lost *Russian School Children* to thieves shortly after *Nude* disappeared from the art museum.

When the Saint Louis Art Museum reopened in December 1977, thieves could hardly contain themselves. They began planning a January heist. The new renovations literally created a window of opportunity.

JANUARY 29, 1978 – REMINGTON TAKES A RIDE

On January 29, 1978, the museum hosted a private event, shutting down later than usual. Around 10:30 p.m., three males smashed the newly installed window on the east wing and entered the museum. It was a cold and snowy Sunday. Two witnesses sleighing on Art Hill stopped and watched the robbery as they hid behind a tree, away from danger.

The thieves entered the window into Gallery 203. The target was just around the corner in Gallery 218, the location of Fredric Remington's bronze sculpture, *Bronco Buster*. Remington, better known for his American cowboy–themed paintings, rarely produced sculptures. The value of this piece climbed, hitting $50,000 in 1978. At least one thief smashed the glass case, grabbed the statue, and headed back to the broken window in Gallery 203.

When thieves returned to 203, the point of entry, they broke display cases containing three more sculptures by unknown artists. A wooden carving of St. Sebastian and two German bronzes, *Hope* and *Prudence*. The wood sculpture was worth the least at $5,000. The $34,500 combined value was derived from their antiquity and craftsmanship.[3]

The two guards on duty were preoccupied or too far away to hear the glass shattering. The new security system, monitored from a central station, detected motion in the gallery. It triggered a silent alarm, and the two guards headed to Sculpture Hall. They shined their flashlights into the east wing gallery. They saw nothing and assumed a false alarm.

Neither guard entered the gallery space for a deeper inspection, so it was unknown whether they would have stumbled upon the three thieves. The instinct to not enter might have saved their lives, but it would not save their jobs.

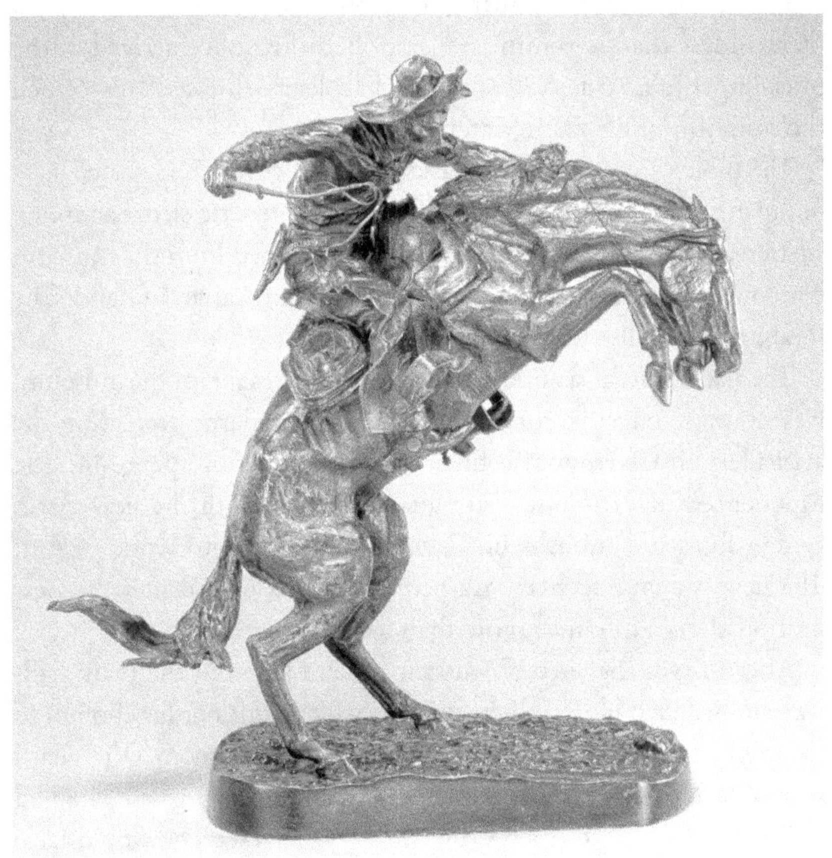

The Bronco Buster *(1895, cast 1907)*
By Fredric Remington, American, 1861–1909
Bronze; 23 × 21½ × 13 inches
Saint Louis Art Museum, Gift of J. Lionberger Davis 201:1955
The main target of the January 29, 1978, theft.

After the robbery, witnesses attempted to wave down a nearby city police patrol car. The police did not see them or misunderstood the waving to be from friendly sledders on Art Hill. The witnesses left the park, drove to the nearest place (a fast-food restaurant), and called the police.

The new alarm detected the motion as soon as the thieves broke the window, alerting security. It recorded the event, which took place in less than two minutes. Yet when the police arrived at the museum, the guards were surprised to learn thieves had robbed the museum under their watch.

The three thieves wore ski masks and U.S. Navy-style pea coats, a popular fashion in 1978. They left behind a generic sledgehammer, shattered glass, and no fingerprints. They emerged from the museum window, pane-less from the break-in, with four statues in hand. The total haul was close to $100,000.

The alarm system, a $600,000 or more investment for the museum, was no more effective than the less expensive alarm protecting the art gallery in Clayton, also hit in a smash-and-run operation. The experienced nighttime security guards worked with the new alarm system for a few months but lacked the training to work *with* it. The new system effectively trained the guards to consider the new motion alerts a nuisance more than a security breach.

After thieves triggered the alarm, a guard stood in the main hallway and wielded his flashlight into the gallery, but not far enough to see the location of the broken window in the last room. The guard would have passed the room with the missing Remington if he had walked far enough to reach Gallery 203. Once there, he would have also discovered the shattered glass and the point of intrusion.

Just months earlier, guards relied on casual strolls throughout the galleries, shining their flashlights into halls and listening for unusual sounds. The same approach triggered a false alarm under the new security system.

A museum security job paid a small hourly wage and primarily attracted retirees or college students. The night shift would have typically been an uneventful, dull evening. Anyone in that position might have read, played music, or even taken a nap to pass the time. No one had ever broken into the museum to burglarize it over its entire existence…until that Sunday evening in January.

The theft overshadowed the well-received museum renovation. Museum leadership had to be disappointed in the loss, security staff response, and the expensive alarm system. Embarrased by the theft, they fired the two evening guards and the security director retired.

FEBRUARY 20, 1978 – GONE IN SIXTY SECONDS

Museum staffers announced they were taking additional precautions to secure the museum's treasures. Either they failed to quickly deploy them, or they were not effective. On February 20, twenty-two short days after the first break-in, thieves returned. They broke the tempered glass panel of the new east wing access door, this time with no witnesses.

The art thieves entered the museum around 8:24 p.m. Once again, the alarm told the new guards of the breach as it tracked the thieves' entry point and motion. This time the robbery took less than sixty seconds.

When guards responded to the east wing door alarm, they saw the tempered glass on the floor and the empty pane. The guards used their flashlights to inspect the galleries. They were convinced it was just an attempted theft.

Police arrived at 8:37 p.m. The guards reassured the officers that nothing was missing. Twelve hours passed before the morning custodian made his way into Gallery 213, where he found three empty pedestals. This time thieves got away with three Auguste Rodin statues with a total value of $45,000.[4]

Rodin was a renowned sculptor, and most people recognize his famous work, *The Thinker*. The three missing Rodins were *The Clenched Hand, Eustache de Saint-Pierre*, and *Jean d'Aire*. The latter two were small bronze models made for the life-size sculpture *Burghers of Calais*, installed in France.[5] All three bronze sculptures were located on the second floor of the east wing, as was the Remington taken in January.

Gallery 213 ran along the south wall. It was long and narrow and displayed nine sculptures between two slender passageways. Thieves bypassed the large sculptures, which were too big to take. The three Rodins were small, unprotected, and only secured with a small protrusion, meant to prevent tipping if touched.

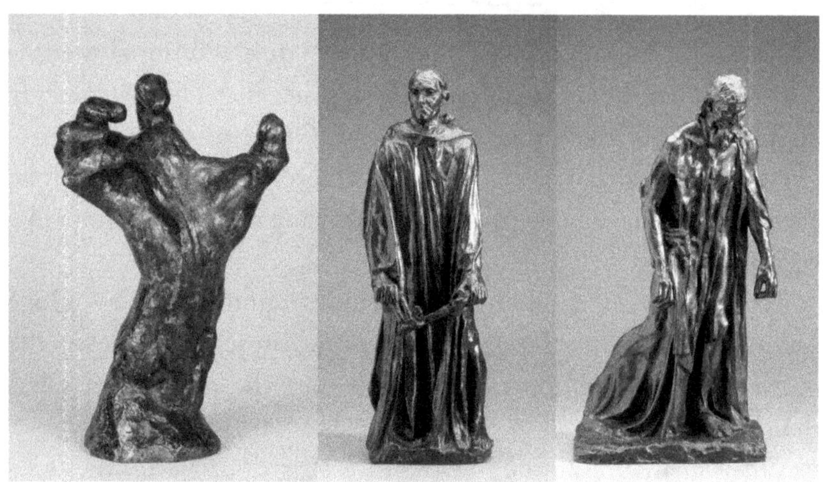

Three bronze sculptures By Auguste Rodin, French, 1840–1917.
Saint Louis Art Museum

The Clenched Hand *(c. 1885); 18⅛ × 10⅜ × 8¼ inches; Funds given by Lanlee Realty Company 3:1957.* Jean d'Aire *(c.1895) 18⁵⁄₁₆ × 5⅞ × 6¹⁄₁₆ inches;* Eustache de Saint-Pierre *(1902–1903) 18½ × 9⅝ × 5¹⁵⁄₁₆ inches; both gifts of Sarah Jane May Waldheim, Mary Kay Waldheim Lemmon, and Lesley Ann Waldheim, in memory of Morton J. May 31 and 29:1984, respectively.*

From Sculpture Hall, the guards would have seen the entire gallery, including the second narrow opening where the thief had entered 213. Immediately to the thief's left, *The Clenched Hand* sat on the first pedestal. A few steps away to his right, the *Burghers of Calais* were together on the second pedestal.

The new guards did not fare much better in reaction, though the museum spared them the fate of their former peers. They managed to keep their jobs and get training courtesy of the police. The police chief was so angered he sent an officer from his robbery division to provide professional instruction to the staff. Then, to step up the police presence on Art Hill, he ordered his patrolmen to park at the art museum when it was time to write their daily reports.[6]

The renovations added a host of new opportunities for the guards. The art on display grew substantially, covering more space than ever in the museum. The side doors and windows added new access points. Anyone, including thieves, could now quickly and easily move from gallery to gallery, even in darkness. The gallery walls that made it hard for even daytime visitors to maneuver around the museum were gone. In 1978, daytime thefts became impossible, and nighttime thefts became possible.

Not once did guards turn on the museum lights immediately following the alarms to look for missing art. Instead, they walked around with flashlights as they had done thousands of times on the evening shift. Those same flashlights failed to shine a light on three empty pedestals in Gallery 213.

The burglars might have stayed away if the museum had left the lights on at night. The darkness became a cover for the thieves, not a deterrent for their actions. Indeed, it would have been easier for a guard to spot the shattered glass from the first robbery or notice three empty pedestals during the second.

The cost of the new alarm system in 1977 equated to about $2.6 million in 2022. The alarm was capable of detecting the most sophisticated robbery attempts. But no thief descended from the roof skylights or made catlike moves to avoid detection. No one tunneled beneath the museum to access the museum galleries. The men broke the glass, ran to the targets, and just as quickly vanished with the art, all long before the police arrived.

The disturbing reality of art theft arrived at Art Hill. After just three months of the museum's stunning makeover, the city added a tall, dingy fence around the east wing for security. With this addition, the renovated museum had the grace and charm of a prison wing.

A SIMPLE MASTER PLAN

A professional fencing operation was far less dramatic than anything a screenwriter conjured for the theater. Weeks before thieves first wielded a sledgehammer through the glass window, they visited the newly renovated museum during regular hours. A fence and a thief meandered through the museum's galleries to identify the prize and the path of least resistance for the heist.

Thieves did not need a fancy blueprint of the building. The visitor map would have provided a floor plan of the museum's wings and all available access points to and from the galleries. Better yet, the map was free to take home and share with accomplices.

The map showed the newly open basement gallery as level one, bearing gallery numbers in the 100 range. The main doors took visitors directly into the second galleries, renumbered in the 200 range. The new windows let natural light into the second floor in the daytime and occasional moonlight at night. The east wing's new window and the recommissioned exit-only door became two entry locations for thieves.

With a starting point and path to the prize, they needed to understand the guard's reaction to the alarm. After museum operating hours, thieves intentionally triggered the silent alarm, carefully timing guard response.

Police speculated that both thefts were committed on orders. In the first robbery, detectives surmised the thieves took the last three statues in gallery 203 on impulse, not as part of a plan.

The men may have encountered an obstacle preventing them from getting to the Rodin bronzes the first time they hit the museum. The Rodin figures were in the same wing and located a short distance from the Remington. In fact, the Rodin sculptures would have been relatively quick and quiet to grab in the first heist because they were not encased.

When the guards flashed their lights into the galleries that January evening, they may have unknowingly forced the thieves to leave behind the Rodins. They headed for the broken window, where they grabbed the most convenient replacements, albeit lesser-valued statues of unknown artists.

If true, the second heist was a return effort to complete the initial order. The thief used a closer entry point to the Rodins and knew their location *precisely*. The second theft took half the time of the first.

The most expensive piece of art was not always the most practical approach. Some investigators expressed their opinion about skipping more valuable art as a sign of immaturity about art knowledge. In reality, the thieves knew exactly what they were doing. Eluding guards while running with a large painting or heavy statue did not fit their modus operandi. Multiple small statues were very wise choices for a thief racing against time.

Taking lesser-known works of famous artists was typical of the period. The pieces could inconspicuously move into other markets to a shady dealer and then be sold to unsuspecting buyers. A fence might patiently wait for a buyer, but a thief expected immediate payment for the goods.

A sense of panic had to have set in among the museum board and administrators, knowing only five years had passed since a thief had taken *Nude* from the museum. By 1978, the missing Picasso oil painting was worth $150,000, five grand more than the total of the seven missing sculptures taken in the two nighttime robberies. The fate of the Remington and Rodin statuaries looked to be statistically in favor of the thieves.

FINALLY, A BREAK NOT INVOLVING GLASS

Seven days after the second museum robbery, police entered the premises of a tiny home on Vest Avenue to take a repeat felon into custody. The FBI had issued a federal warrant charging him with an interstate flight to avoid prosecution for a jewelry robbery he committed in Illinois.[7]

At just twenty-five, John Crabtree* already had an extensive criminal record. His criminal history revealed a rap sheet from 1968, when he was just fifteen. Crabtree was out of prison for a short period, having recently served a fourteen-month burglary sentence at the Missouri State Penitentiary. Before that, he had three separate convictions for burglaries in Kentucky.

While in custody, he confessed to his involvement in both museum burglaries. Crabtree claimed it was so easy the first time that he returned on his own a second time. He knew what to steal and who could move it. He may have acted on his own accord the second time around, but at minimum, he knew who would buy the Rodin statues.

Arrested on a different charge, then admitting to another crime, meant one of two things: Police may have forced a confession, or more likely, Crabtree offered information about the art robbery to negotiate a deal. Police returned to the house on Vest Avenue. They located the least valuable of the stolen pieces, the statue of St. Sebastian, in the garage. The tip of the saint's finger had broken off and been left behind in the trunk of Crabtree's car. The evidence sealed his involvement in the museum robbery.

Crabtree explained to the police that he was part of a four-member smash-and-run gang that hit the museum. A similar hit was used to steal *Russian School Children* from the Clayton gallery in 1973 and the Lindbergh statues from the history museum in early 1974.

Someone paid Crabtree and his gang to steal art. Perhaps they even provided the white 1965 Chevy Impala with missing plates witnesses identified in the January robbery. Hired thieves protected the criminal layers up the chain, including the fences. Behind the fences, a criminal distribution network waited to move the stolen art to the hands of a shady art dealer, crime boss, or ignorant private collector.

The police initially identified two arrests to the media but only mentioned Crabtree's name. The investigating officer referred to the second accomplice as the "unnamed informant" to disguise his identity. The unnamed informant was likely the second robber of three to enter the museum in January.

Police learned of the third gang member involved in the first museum robbery, Chuck Gant*. Gant died from a bullet wound to the head two days before the second robbery at the museum. The reported motive for his death was an unfair split of the loot from a pawn shop robbery. The killer had no involvement in the museum robbery, but police apprehended him a day before police arrested Crabtree.

A fourth member of the smash-and-run gang, Stan Williams*, had been in for questioning for the museum break-ins. Police knew him to also be an associate of Crabtree. The circuit attorney said they had information that he had been a conspirator in the art case, having planned the heist or transferred the stolen objects.

Police thought Williams was too old to commit the robbery. They assumed his role was as the middleman between the gang and the lowest link of the fencing operation, repeat suspect Robert Meier.

The gang hired to steal art was the first evidence of a fencing operation targeting the museum. The racket deployed nonmember associates of organized crime, multiple degrees removed from the person who initiated the order. By design, Crabtree was never told who ordered the Remington or where it was going. It was a layer of protection for those higher up in the fencing racket and, ultimately, those pulling the strings.

Crabtree and the unnamed informant advised police that Meier still possessed the art, stating he was unable to get rid of the pieces because of the heat. The police showed up at his home with a search warrant. Police had arrested Meier several times before, though they never could prosecute him due to lack of evidence,[8] a common problem with prosecuting anyone for theft in the 1970s.

With a warrant in hand, police forced open the door after the occupants refused entry. The officers found quite a stash of purloined items. It took an army truck to haul the stolen goods from Meier's home to the police station.

Police recovered over 130 pinched items from the home search with a total value above $300,000. The looted art included Rockwell lithographs and a Wayne Cooper painting identified by police as stolen from the Clayton gallery in July 1976. Among the haul of expensive oriental rugs were jade and a copy of a Rembrandt painting.[9]

But Meier knew better than to store something as hot as the remaining six bronzes at home. The stash had no missing statues from the art museum. Nor would officers discover a cold storage room containing *Russian School Children* or *Nude*.

Meier faced a criminal charge in St. Louis city for his involvement in the art museum robbery and another in St. Louis County for the stolen merchandise from the Clayton gallery recovered in his home.

Five years earlier, Meier bragged to Kelly that he would never talk no matter what evidence he faced or who asked the questions.[10] Suspiciously, after his arrest, police told the media a "very influential person" was behind the January theft of the Remington.[11]

The ambiguous description behind the order could have been the crime boss or a respected businessman. Meier would likely have been the only person arrested to know who was behind the demand for the *Bronco Buster*. And if he had talked, would he have given a real name or a false lead to protect himself and the identity of others higher up in the operation?

RECOVERY OF STOLEN ART

St. Louis Circuit Attorney George Peach made a critical decision about the art theft case. He weighed the evidence available to prosecute a fence against the effort it would take to get the statues returned to the museum. Peach and St. Louis Metropolitan Police Department Captain Wallace* worked to recover the art, even though the theft fell under FBI jurisdiction. Their negotiations would bring back the remaining six bronzes in three separate returns.[12]

Captain Wallace received the first anonymous tip at his home at 10:10 p.m. on March 11. The female caller said he could find the two small bronzes from the first museum robbery at the Quality Inn Motel on Oakland Avenue, room 204. The police arrived by eleven that night and located a box containing *Hope* and *Prudence* in a washroom. Police believed the name on the hotel room was likely fictitious and dismissed it as evidence.[13]

Forensics found the two small bronzes rubbed in oil and free of fingerprints. The two least-valuable bronzes were returned as a sign of "good gesture," implying a negotiation between police and those holding the goods.

Soon after police recovered *Hope* and *Prudence* from the hotel, thieves demanded a ransom for the return of the Remington and the Rodin bronzes. A month passed before the subsequent recovery of the other pieces occurred.

On April 7, Captain Wallace received another anonymous tip at his home at 8:30 p.m. on a Friday. A male voice said, "Something you are looking for is in a Goodwill box at Forest Park and Sarah," referring to the cross streets. Police found the *Bronco Buster* wrapped in a garbage bag, laid in the used clothes box behind a gated area. The Remington statue, stolen in the first heist, was the most valuable of all the stolen statues. Like *Hope* and *Prudence*, thieves covered the figure in oil to prevent the detection of fingerprints.[14]

Peach's account of the recovery of the stolen bronzes included a report that the Remington was in Detroit at one point.[15] The St. Louis LCN had familial ties with members of the Detroit crime family. The two bosses of the St. Louis and Detroit crime families went to prison for conspiring to hide their investment in the Frontier casino. (Coincidentally, the St. Louis boss had just been released near the museum's grand reopening in December.) Perhaps the statue really moved to Detroit. It could explain the month delay between the first recovery and the return of the Remington.

On April 9, one day after police recovered the *Bronco Buster* behind Goodwill, the captain took his last anonymous call at 10:30 Saturday evening. A male voice directed him to the rear yard of Fisher Metals on Manchester Road. He and other officers went to the location and climbed a tall fence to retrieve the statues from the yard. Two Rodin statues were in a pillowcase up against the gate, and they found the *Clenched Hand* in a truck trailer used to haul scrap metal. All three bronzes were in good shape.[16]

I highly doubt ransom was the initial motivation for the robbery. First, ransom motives were usually behind art thefts of a much larger value than the entire lot stolen in the two 1978 art heists. Second, with multiple people in custody talking, the art was a liability and challenging to sell. Third, sending the Remington to Detroit to execute a local ransom scheme made no sense, so this scheme had to be an afterthought.

Only a few months had passed since the Chicago OCSF took down a similar fencing operation in St. Louis. This could have provided the police with additional insight into the criminal network. The repeat media exposure of the statues stolen in 1978 made them too risky to sell in another market or pass through customs. I believe ransom was one last attempt to cash in on the heist and bleed money from the museum.

Peach expressed publicly he did not want to see the pieces destroyed. He weighed the odds of prosecution against returning the art to the museum—items that he described as irreplaceable. A ransom may have been paid, or he could have agreed not to press charges when he negotiated the return. Catching a fence required more evidence. In 1978, the odds of sending a fence to jail were still in favor of the fence, despite the success of the RICO Act.

The art museum had all seven statues back safely with minimal damage, but the case of stolen art wouldn't die in the media.

THE FISHER FRAME JOB

With Crabtree and Meier's arrests and the final recovery of the statues, the case seemed closed. Yet finding the Rodins at Fisher Metals, a scrap metal business, would add another twist to the 1978 museum heist. Someone chose the location to frame the president of Fisher Metals, and it almost worked.

Tracy Fisher* had been the target of arson, violence, and attempts on his life in the previous two years. He said the attacks came from the orders of a local business enemy.[17] Someone desired to force Fisher out of business or into business with organized crime.

Scrapyards were depicted in movies as an ideal setting for criminal activity. The metal crusher was fitting for a big-screen Mafia whack. But in real life, organized crime figures were likely attracted to scrapyard businesses for financial purposes. Local scrapyards operated under a "no questions asked" policy. Fisher Metals was an unregulated business that dealt in cash, ideal for money laundering.

An hour or so before the tip that sent police to Fisher Metals, Fisher's antique store had been broken into. Fisher believed thieves first attempted to plant the Rodins at the store, at least until the store's alarm sounded. He said responding police must have scared them off, forcing the robbers to place the Rodins at the scrapyard.[18] Leaving behind the stolen Rodins on the shelf of an antique storefront was a reasonable, thought-out effort that could have succeeded in framing Fisher as being involved.

The day after police searched Meier's home, the local newspapers printed mugshots of Meier and Crabtree. Fisher recognized the two associates as working for his "business enemy," a name he didn't share with the press. He must have provided the information to the FBI, as they were actively investigating the past assaults.

Crabtree attempted to kill Fisher in 1977 during a shakedown. The assailant's gun jammed, resulting in a pistol-whipping instead.[19] The scrapyard owner pointed to Meier as the man who likely intended to frame him for the robbery. The observation was closer to the truth than Fisher was capable of knowing.

Meier shared a similar tactic in 1973 with FBI informant Kelly when he considered robbing the history museum. His proposed scheme would use stolen artifacts from the Jefferson Memorial to "frame his enemies."[20]

Despite the ongoing FBI investigation and Fisher identifying the suspects, the St. Louis police were convinced Fisher was somehow involved in the heist. They arrested him the day after police recovered the Rodins. The judge let Fisher go as there was no evidence to support his involvement in the crime. He filed an official complaint against the St. Louis city police for false arrest.

Fisher never named his business enemy in public. After digging through some more government archives, I could narrow Fisher's rival down to a local owner of Schafer Vending. The government pegged Schafer* as an associate of the local Mafia boss. Schafer was "convicted of using professional enforcers to bomb businesses who refused to use his vending machines and engaging in a conspiracy with an official to extort money from his competitors."[21]

Various sources pointed to Crabtree and Williams working directly for Schafer or indirectly through Meier.[22] Police described Williams as Meier's right-hand man and the muscle used to get others to change (or not) vending machine companies.[23] In other words, he was a middle-aged enforcer who also worked for Fisher's business enemy.

The story continued with one more strange turn. Less than two weeks after the art recovery, Crabtree and the unnamed informant in his robbery gang refused to testify against Meier. Without their testimonies, the prosecutor's case weakened. On April 27, the St. Louis district attorney dropped the charges against Meier in the art museum robbery.

St. Louis County also dropped its case against Meier for the gallery items stolen and recovered on his property in March. The prosecutor's office in Clayton notified witnesses not to appear in court because the case against Meier was weak. Too much time had passed between the theft and the recovery—one more example of the problem with laws involving the possession of stolen property.

Williams met with the FBI at the end of May then disappeared a week later. On June 11, an Illinois farmer found Williams' charred body while plowing a field in Alton, a small town just across the river northeast of St. Louis City. It took a week for authorities to identify the prints of the remaining fingers that failed to burn. He had been shot with two different guns, a sign that maybe more than one assailant murdered Williams.[24]

Authorities never caught Williams' killer(s). The attempt to get information through the Freedom of Information Act (FOIA) failed as the FBI destroyed the records in routine purging. The murder was destined to remain unsolved, and Williams was one more casualty connected to the 1978 art museum robbery.

The museum acknowledged the investigating police as heroes for recovering the stolen statues. By midsummer, the investigation into Fisher's arrest cleared the police officers of wrongdoing. Months later, Fisher sold his business and moved to Florida.

Despite the enormous publicity and mayhem surrounding the last set of art thefts at the museum, it was not enough to preserve the case files for historical reference. After requesting the files from the police archives and the FBI, both responded that the case files were no longer available.

I was disappointed to learn the files were not considered historical records. After all, the 1978 art thefts led to the discovery of the local plot to kill a civil rights leader, which became documented history.

THE ST. LOUIS CONSPIRACIES

Police named Meier as the "mastermind" behind the local art thefts, pinning him as the lowest link in the chain. They implied there was another player, the next link in the chain, thought to be the main fence for some of the bronzes.

Wallace and Peach zoomed in on one suspect as the leading fence capable of moving some of the stolen statues from the museum. Wallace said they had been chasing this fence for many years, but they could never "nail him, maybe that's why he moved to Chicago." Without ever releasing his name, the newspaper described the suspected fence as someone indicted for planning a 1972 jewelry heist.[25]

It was unmistakably a description of Kelly. He became an informant after the 1972 jewelry heist, developed a relationship with Meier, and then reported on Meier's activity to his FBI handler for eight months in 1974. Kelly moved to Chicago after his stint as an FBI snitch ended in 1975.

Right before the January museum heist, Kelly's Chicago gallery ran classified ads asking for bronze sculptures.[26] After the heist, the ad copy advertised "MUSEUM" quality pieces for sale.[27] The ads were an odd coincidence or perhaps evidence that supported police suspicion about Kelly being part of a fencing operation moving stolen goods from St. Louis to Chicago.

Local authorities suspected Kelly and Meier had worked together. The relationship did not seem likely in light of the information Kelly reported to the FBI in 1974. Yet police suspicion led FBI agents to run a background check on Kelly.

In Kelly's FBI file, they discovered the five-page informant memorandum his handler recorded after their meeting in March 1974. The document pointed to Meier, who bridged the Rockwell heist at the Clayton gallery in 1973, the history museum robbery in 1974, the 1976 gallery theft, and the fall 1978 art museum robberies.

The FBI or STLPD purged the case files on local stolen art because they lacked significant content to justify preservation. This made Kelly's informant file the only investigative document on local art thefts to survive the decade. It solidified a fencing operation stealing local art from the museum and galleries that existed when *Nude* disappeared.

In 2017, the government released the memo with no redactions, a gift from the universe at a time when routine purges closed all doors to the '70s art thefts. It provided the missing link between multiple art robberies that gave credence to the theory that *Nude* could have been lifted in an organized crime fencing operation.

The same universal mojo was at work in 1978. As police investigated the museum heist, the House Select Committee on Assassinations (HSCA) convened for something far from art theft. They began investigating numerous conspiracies behind the murders of two prominent figures: President John F. Kennedy and Dr. Martin Luther King, Jr. The objective was to decide if their killers were lone assassins or part of a greater conspiracy involving other players.

As Peach and Wallace worked to get the art back into the museum's hands, the FBI had begun their own in inquiry into Meier's assassination claim found in Kelly's informant file. The FBI reported the information to the HSCA committee, which sent investigators to the homes of Meier, Kelly, and Spacanelli, inquiring about what they might know about the claim.

The citizens of St. Louis had no idea the saga of the art museum robberies that began in late January, and finally resolved in May, was leading to a more devious story. Despite the enormous local coverage of the St. Louis art thefts, it would be an out-of-town newspaper to break the story about an assassination plot to kill King.

The New York Times released the bombshell to the public in July 1978. The HSCA intentionally exposed the story months before the public hearings. *The NY Times* interviewed Meier and unveiled the rest of the bones of the conspiracy established in the 1974 memo. Meier claimed two St. Louis area men made him an offer of $50,000 between late 1966 and early 1967 to assassinate, or hire an assassin, to kill King. Both men were already dead by 1978 and couldn't defend the accusations. (*That* burden was left to their widows.)

By then, the local prosecution had dropped the art theft charges against Meier. The suspect also negotiated immunity from the claims contained in the memo before he agreed to testify about the offer. The story spread across American newspapers and gained coverage as the HSCA prepared for the public hearings later that year. The museum art theft became the closing reference to how the FBI discovered the assassination plot.

What proceeded after unleashing the claim was a lot to unpack. I'll provide the condensed version of the hearing, summarized from public records. Like the story of the missing Picasso, it was a fascinating local event most of my generation had never heard of. It also provided a peek into the dangerous operations of an organized crime fencing scheme and why the FBI memo about stolen art became a piece of history.

On the heels of the art robbery, the FBI and HSCA investigators wanted Kelly to answer questions about what he reported in 1974. Kelly provided the information in confidence to his FBI handler. In the infamous FBI memo, Kelly swore to never testify to the information he provided on Meier if asked.

The memo's content, which basically ratted out Meier, would have been highly uncomfortable, considering Kelly and Meier were suspected accomplices in the 1978 museum heist. Kelly agreed to meet with the FBI but didn't bother to show up on the advice of his lawyers. He kept his promise and refused to testify to the HSCA about statements he provided years earlier.[28]

The committee investigators quickly sought someone who could corroborate Meier's claim. They started with the list of players called out in the memo, starting with Meier's brother-in-law, Spacanelli.

Spacanelli was arrested for a contract killing and served his time in the Missouri State Penitentiary. He and Ray shared the same cell block. This gave credence to the HSCA theory that Meier passed along the offer to Spacanelli, who passed the information to Ray in 1966 or early 1967 before Ray escaped.

The HSCA privately interviewed Spacanelli, but a court sealed his testimony until 2027. Spacanelli denied the allegation in the media and said he only knew of Ray but never spoke with him while serving their sentences. Spacanelli and Meier denied ever having a conversation about the contract; therefore, Spacanelli couldn't have passed it to Ray.

Once again, the committee seemed to have struck out. They knew Meier's criminal history made him a questionable witness. They asked him to name other people he shared the offer with to corroborate his testimony. He gave the committee the name of two lawyers, and one was Monte Randolph.

Meier testified he told Randolph of the contract offer on two separate occasions, first in 1968 and again in 1974. Attorney-client privilege protected the information from surfacing sooner, and both parties had to waive these rights for testimony.

When Kelly's informant report resurfaced, Randolph was a judge in St. Louis. Judge Randolph wanted nothing to do with Meier or the committee. Randolph was up for reelection when Meier gave his name to HSCA investigators. To Randolph's dismay, the HSCA subpoenaed him to testify in November 1978.

The committee's questions took Randolph back to his earliest encounters with Meier. After Randolph left the Morris Shenker law firm, he opened a private law practice in 1968. One of his earliest client records showed he registered Meier's new business venture, a vending company. This was the first opportunity for Meier to speak to Randolph about the offer. The judge confirmed the 1968 meeting but didn't recall discussing Meier's contract offer on King.

Randolph only confirmed hearing the story in 1974 after he settled Meier's civil case over missing vending equipment. He said after the case, they were meandering in the court halls, and Meier took him aside and asked how immunity worked.

Then, to discredit his own testimony, Randolph presented a new theory. He believed Meier planted the story with Kelly to expose Kelly as an FBI informant. Randolph suggested that if the FBI questioned Meier, it would confirm Kelly as someone Meier could not trust. Randolph had his reasons for pitching a new theory to the HSCA. Fortunately, it became a permanent record and one more source connecting a fencing operation targeting high-value items to local organized crime.

To explain his new theory, Randolph offered other details about the 1972 jewelry heist, the crime that made Kelly an FBI informant. The $250,000 of looted jewelry was sold through the Mafia network in Louisiana and Arkansas. The final sale was to a top boss in

Shreveport, Louisiana and the suspects transported the gems via a charted plane serviced by the Little Rock, Arkansas police.[29]

The heist occurred seven months before *Nude* disappeared from the art museum. If anything, it confirmed the fencing operation moved their loot to members of organized crime, not just storefronts.

Randolph told the committee that his testimony, and the public testimony of others, put their lives in danger (referring to himself, Kelly, and Meier). Randolph believed the person who purchased the stolen statues from the museum would come after them. As evidence, he pointed to Williams, who talked with the FBI a week before he showed up dead. [30]

It was a bold claim, one the HSCA would ignore. The testimonies would continue and become public information in the 1979 final report. When the hearings wrapped, the HSCA publicly released four white supremacist theories linked to two local men who also died years before the hearings. In each one, Ray allegedly received word of the $50,000 offer to kill King—the same offer Meier declined somewhere around 1966 or 1967.[31]

Ray's lawyers saw the theories as a misdirection to shift blame away from a government conspiracy to kill King. Under J. Edgar Hoover's watch, Ray's supporters pointed to the FBI as the conspirator and Ray as a mere patsy.[32]

The hearings were in 1978; Hoover was dead, and William Webster had just become the third FBI director in its history. Webster, the federal judge who oversaw the 1972 jewelry heist case, had been thrust into a hearing where Ray's team pointed to the FBI as the conspirator behind King's death.

The HSCA concluded that Ray did not act on his own, but they pointed to the St. Louis-based conspiracy as the most likely reason for the assassination of the civil rights leader.[33]

The FBI and St. Louis theories can be seen at the National Civil Rights Museum in Memphis, Gallery 2. The building eerily preserved the room where the assassin allegedly fired the shot, ultimately killing King.

The FBI memo led to the St. Louis-based conspiracy and guaranteed its preservation as historical evidence in a national investigation that set out to disprove the lone assassin theory in King's murder. But the memo also provided insight into other local art thefts in c.1973 and birthed my own St. Louis conspiracy: *Nude's* disappearance was likely under orders from the local Mafia.

10

CHAPTER

The Pro vs. the Amateur

FROM THE HISTORY OF THE OTHER ART THEFTS, I could better understand the local fencing operation that could have been responsible for lifting and moving *Nude*. News sources, FBI documents, and other government records tied the gallery and museum robberies between June 1973 and February 1978 to the same fencing operation. Below summarizes the information collected and how the fencing operation worked that could have moved the missing Picasso. At least two St. Louis fencing operations stole art, and the central characters of each had one or more links to the local Mafia.

The fencing group busted in 1977 had focused on stealing high-valued goods from residential homes. The local man, Ellis, known for his safecracking skills, led a team of thieves on night raids across multiple states. They broke into residential locations and stole art, jewelry, and antiques. Ellis rented a local apartment solely for storing the valuable loot until items could be safely moved to another location.

Cold storage was a common trait of both fencing operations. The stolen Rockwell had allegedly went into cold storage until it eventually moved to and landed in the hands of a couple in New Orleans.

The second fencing operation focused on public locations like museums, galleries, and related businesses. This team hired thieves and provided explicit instructions on what to take. The thieves committed the theft after hours, broke the glass to gain entry, took the required item, and exchanged it for a predetermined fee. The fence planned and executed the heists but did not partake in the physical robbery.

Thieves stole from museums and galleries under direct instructions from the lowest link. This leg of the operation focused on quality over quantity, sporadically targeting high-valued items that had to be distributed to other cities. The press was likelier to splash a museum robbery on the front page of a newspaper, making it risky to sell it locally.

Museum thefts in the United States were rare compared to other venues because museums usually had 24/7 security. It made sense that targeting a museum would come from someone further up the fencing food chain. If someone high in the hierarchy ordered the theft, like the bronze Remington, stolen art skipped local storage and quickly made its way through the network to its final destination.

The fence would not share information about who ordered the item as a part of a safety net that protected everyone in the chain. However, the order that sent thieves busting into galleries could have come from anywhere in the chain, including the lowest fencing link.

Months after police raided Meier's home and took a truckload of stolen goods to the station, Meier's family filed a formal complaint to police. They asked for the goods to be returned to their home. It demonstrated that not all heists were for the Syndicate's direct benefit. Fences also had expensive tastes that their legal fronts likely didn't financially support. By the way, the police returned the stolen items seized in the raid to the verified owners.

If the Mafia was behind the order to steal *Nude* in 1973, it was on demand from a higher power. The Syndicate fencing operation would have been the most likely reason for the theft of *Nude,* but the players who executed the heist were likely different than in 1978. Kelly and Meier didn't know each other in April 1973 according to the informant memo, so they certainly were not working together to steal *Nude*.

I was still not sure who took it directly under the noses of security, museum staff, and visitors on the afternoon of April 11, 1973. However, if taken for financial gain, *Nude* needed a fencing operation in St. Louis to move it to another city.

Several news reports of thieves purloining private collections of Picasso art occurred months after the artist died. Thieves took Picasso's art in Maine, Texas, and New York, and all of the thefts were economically motivated. *Nude* had the unfortunate title of being the first painting stolen from a museum after the artist died.

Economic benefits can motivate anyone to steal art. Picasso had died only a few days before, so *Nude* was bound to rise in value. The painting hung on a temporary wall close to the main museum exit. With no perimeter alarm to protect it, anyone could have grabbed *Nude* and slipped it into an oversized purse, a briefcase, or a jacket. The circumstances were a perfect scenario for a lone opportunist. However, even a greedy individual needed the help of a professional fencing network to move art, which was readily available in 1973.

The only way to know if a lone opportunist moved *Nude* through the fencing operation was to ask someone who might have direct knowledge of a fencing operation from the period. Maybe they remembered the theft or could provide intelligent speculation on where it might have gone or who wanted it.

The number of people with direct knowledge of the St. Louis art thefts had dwindled. The professional safecracker involved with the

1977 federal bust died in 1983. The men who directly robbed the museum had all perished. In recent years, only one associate named in the last museum heist ever talked to the press. I hoped he would speak again, but this time about what he might have heard or remembered about the theft of *Nude.*

I reached out to Meier, fully expecting to hear a long, high-pitched tone signaling an out-of-service phone number. To my surprise, he answered the phone. After a brief introduction outlining my purpose for the call, we began to chat.

I anticipated a repentant soul having reflected on his long life: an elderly gentleman willing to reveal the truth behind the mysteries of the St. Louis art thefts.

What I found was an aged fence looking to run one more scheme. He asked if I could get him a publisher willing to pay upfront cash for his story. Meier gave a similar response to a news reporter who asked about the Rockwell theft during the 2007 legal battle over ownership. He was only willing to share his story *after* receiving payment. He said he could not put his story in a manuscript pitch because a publisher could steal it.

The story he wanted to tell could have been interesting, or it could have been a regurgitation of the information already available in the public records. Either way, I was interested in the Picasso and continued to explain that was the focus I planned for the book. His first reaction to whether he had heard about the theft of *Nude* reflected genuine surprise. He answered with a question of his own: "Picasso? I never heard about that."

At first, I found it difficult to believe a man who likely scoured the paper for gallery exhibits to plan his next heist would have failed to have read the stories of a Picasso stolen from the museum, especially one that took place just two months before *Russian School Children* disappeared. But then again, *Nude* had always been an elusive painting.

Not knowing whether I could believe his response, I pried further. I asked about the missing Lindbergh busts, taken from the history museum months after the Picasso. He responded with a story about sitting in his favorite restaurant one evening. A waiter, he said, came up to him and gave him a personal message from Anne Lindbergh; she wanted her statues back. Then he denied having her missing sculptures or ever taking them. "Back then, I was blamed for everything," he declared.

Following up with the archivist at the history museum, she doubted the story of Anne having dinner in St. Louis during this period. Charles had cancer in 1974, and Anne likely took care of her husband in their home in Maui, Hawaii.

Meier was as old as Picasso was when the artist died in 1973. He told sporadic tales of crime and celebrity connections in our phone conversation. Perhaps his mental acuity had declined, or he had attention deficit disorder. He could have just been lonely and was thrilled to speak to someone new about his prime years.

He bragged that famed producer Steven Spielberg was planning to make a movie about him. No doubt, his story hinted at his knowledge of the stolen Rockwell that landed in Spielberg's hands. In fact, he stated Spielberg named a character after him in the movie *Bridge of Spies*. The movie character turned out to be an actual historical figure with the same last name as Meier, a complete coincidence.

He shared other strange thoughts, including the shooting of *Hustler* magazine founder Larry Flynt. Meier said Flynt talked too much in his magazine. Flynt was a conspiracy theorist and financially funded some of the investigations into JFK's death. After taking a further look into his story, the timing didn't mesh between the shooting of Flynt and the discovery of a St. Louis plot to assassinate King.

Meier provided no insight to help solve this fifty-year-old mystery. I contemplated our conversations for a few days, trying to determine if he really knew something or not. Some of his stories stretched the imagination, but each reflected the alleged connection to the other art thefts.

Not once did Meier drop a quirky story about the missing Picasso. He never attempted to engage in a conversation about it. While I don't know the exact story he wanted to sell to a publisher, I am confident it didn't involve the missing Picasso.

I reached a dead end with the last local living suspect in the fencing network to last hit the art museum. The theft of *Nude* could have been an organized crime contract theft, but the player(s) remained unknown. The other option was that a lone opportunist stole it and that was why Meier had not recalled the art theft.

INTRINSIC VALUE

Greed has been the assumed motive for *Nude's* disappearance thus far and the most logical explanation for any art theft. Yet a lone opportunist might have stolen *Nude* for its intrinsic value, an emotional connection to the art or artist. There have been rare cases of such thefts in more recent years.

A man from Greece became obsessed with a couple of paintings at an Athens museum, one of which was a Picasso. He stole the works and held them for nine years until his guilt drove him to confess his sins, or perhaps from learning the authorities were on his trail. He buried the lifted pieces in a shallow, rocky area in a gorge on the mainland. The lone opportunist was a forty-year-old construction worker when he stole it. Perhaps a mid-life crisis was also an acceptable reason for stealing art.

Another individual thief stole hundreds of small, valuable pieces from cottages, galleries, and museums. It was an obsession bordering on art kleptomania. His mother was so sick of the artistic "mess" he compiled in her home that she burned the paintings, not realizing their monetary value.

The artist Mark Rothko painted large, abstract blocks of color, which have brought so many people to tears, doctors dubbed the emotional response the "Rothko Effect."[1] Psychologists and neurologists did not have a complete answer for the effect his paintings had on people. His art might have initiated a self-reflective, meditative state, causing extreme emotions to pour out of a gazing viewer's soul.

Though Rothko might be the most famous artist of works that make people cry, others reacted differently to less abstract paintings. Paintings of sad people or serene scenes triggered personal memories, leading to emotional responses just from viewing the art.

Nude was anything but blocks of color like a Rothko. In fact, it had simple black-and-white uneven brushstrokes outlining a kneeling, naked figure. Even the 1934 museum bulletin's description of *Nude* was far more colorful than the painting: "Here the object was not to represent an individual but to use the lines and forms suggested by the figure to make a formal composition which will be beautiful or pleasing in itself with little regard to the figure it suggests."[2]

Crying at artwork went out centuries ago and was rare in the twentieth century. The average museum visitor admired the artwork and quickly moved to the next painting on the wall. The amazement of the technique was appreciated, but not enough to bring just any-one to tears.[3]

An emotional response to art was already rare, and no one ever admitted an urge to steal it after an emotional meltdown. The simple figure of *Nude* lacked color, and it didn't match any of the styles that drove people to tears where people have connected to its intrinsic value.

A lone opportunist stealing *Nude* for intrinsic value was the best chance of the painting remaining in St. Louis and waiting to resurface. The naked figure, awkwardly arranging her hair, might be nonchalantly hanging in someone's bathroom (where most naked people comb their hair), awaiting discovery.

WEIGHING THE MOTIVES

I immediately eliminated motives in the 1973 museum robbery involving ransom, rewards, and nameless billionaires. I concluded *Nude* could not have been in a scheme to recover or hide Nazi-looted art. Unfortunately, I couldn't give the motive of intrinsic value much weight because most of the Picasso thefts after the artist's death were for economic value. After Picasso died, an inevitable increase in value would create demand for his work. Greed still seemed to me to be the best motive for the theft.

In 1976, thieves stole 119 pieces of Picasso's art on exhibit at the former papal palace in France. Authorities tracked and recovered the stolen art, ultimately bound for the United States. The theft validated the apparent demand for Picasso's art in America. *Nude* most likely went to someone stateside and, with any luck, stayed here over the past fifty years.

The five-year span of art thefts that hit St. Louis museums and galleries suddenly stopped. The period of art thefts that started in 1973 and ended in 1978 were bookends of unfortunate days at the Saint Louis Art Museum. Multiple reasons probably contributed to the fencing operation's abrupt ending.

The first blow came to the local residential fencing operation in the fall of 1977. The federal organized crime task force busted the team and recovered over a million dollars in art, jewelry, and antiques stolen from residential properties across multiple states. The top safe-cracker pled guilty to the theft and the racket.

The second blow was the national exposure of the FBI memo and the mayhem that occurred after the last two heists at the Saint Louis Art Museum. The publicity lasted until the rest of the year, then was permanently captured in the 1979 HSCA report and investigation files.

The third factor was a combination of needed changes, which occurred in 1979. The FBI launched the first stolen art database (but without *Nude*), which allowed all agents to access federal reports of stolen art filed anywhere in the US. Missouri tightened its stolen property laws so prosecutors could successfully convict a fence. Local museums and galleries learned from their losses and tightened security to prevent future art thefts.

The final blow delivered to the fencing operation may have been the infighting among local Syndicate figures. The alliance formed years earlier between members of three local factions fell apart. A power struggle over union control led to a 1979 car bomb, killing Meier's brother-in-law, Spacanelli. Then, in 1980, the local La Cosa Nostra leader died of cancer. A host of car bombings followed between members of the local Syndicate operation. Essentially, local Syndicate power waned.

The St. Louis art thefts have been quiet since 1979, excluding a period of private-collection forgeries. (Forgeries, a whole other art scheme for profit, were outside this book's pursuit.) *Nude's* destination in 1973 was most likely domestic, but the painting could have exchanged international hands over the decades. The lack of catalog and database references kept the painting under the radar for too long. I can only hope it fell into the hands of a good-faith buyer or an heir living in the United States.

A LONE OPPORTUNIST OR A MAFIA-ORDERED THEFT?

Nude's provenance forever changed the day it disappeared. If the painting miraculously resurfaced, then the amended history might mention the last (illegal) owner. But the extended travels, beginning with the person(s) behind the theft, would be nothing more than a mysterious provenance gap—a matching bookend to the one before *Nude's* 1934 arrival at the museum.

No one could explain with certainty how Dietz Edzard acquired the Picasso. I could only postulate that *Nude* was one of the missing pieces conned from Picasso's mother in 1930. The timing, the anonymous transaction, and the legal battle that brewed between Picasso and Edzard when it arrived at the museum seemed highly suspicious. Does it prove *Nude* was part of the conned loot or simply an ill-timed sale?

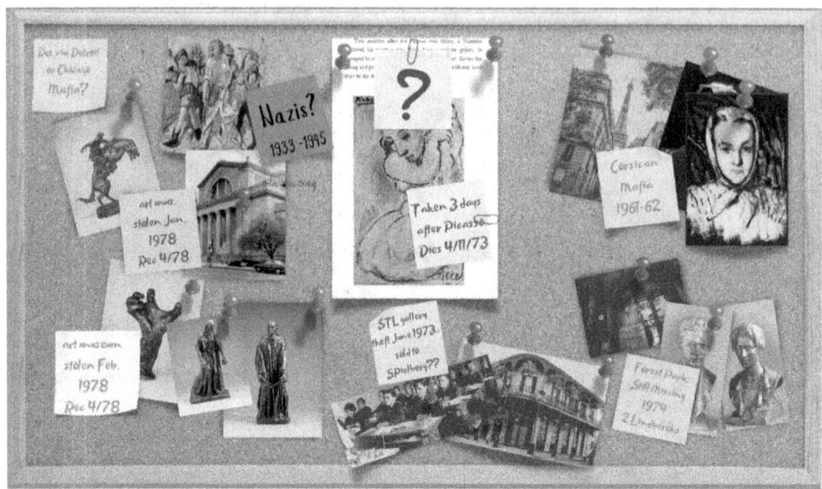

Within a week of the 1973 Picasso robbery, local police were leaning toward a contract hit as the motive. A Washington, DC Interpol investigator said organized criminals were becoming more attracted to art thefts and expected the number to increase. Yet no speculation surfaced in 1978, at least publicly, that the same people that ordered the *Bronco Buster* theft might have also put the contract on *Nude*.

Only two things seemed to be the same about the 1973 and 1978 robberies: 1) thieves took art from the east wing, and 2) law enforcement suspected they were contract thefts (1978 was confirmed). The differences in the crime could also be attributed to museum renovation.

Between 1973 and 1978, the museum's entry points and interior flow changed. The following photos are before and after the 1978 renovation of the east wing, courtesy of Saint Louis Art Museum archives. In the end, the puppet thieves and fences may have changed, but likely not the puppeteer pulling the strings.

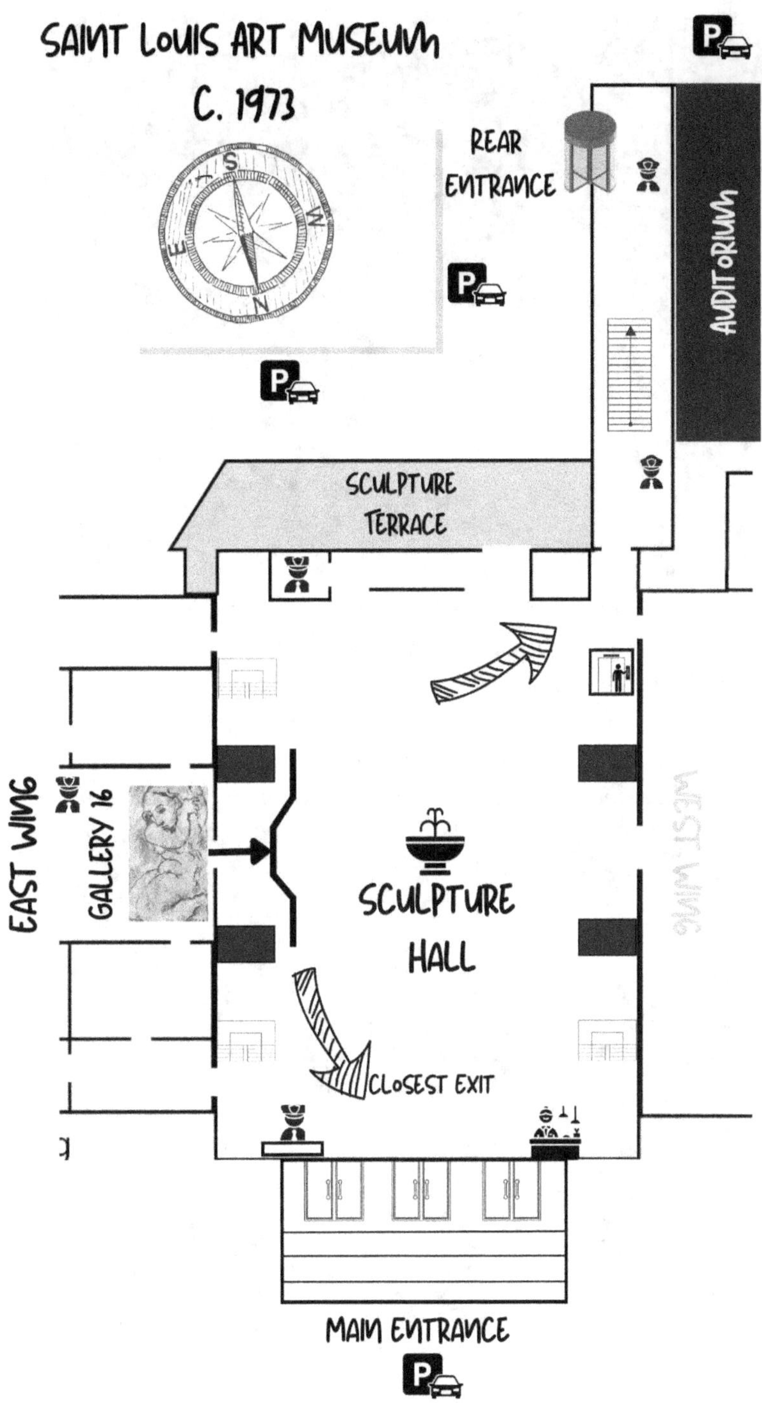
SAINT LOUIS ART MUSEUM
C. 1973
N
S
E
W
REAR ENTRANCE
AUDITORIUM
P
P
P
SCULPTURE TERRACE
EAST WING
WEST WING
GALLERY 16
SCULPTURE HALL
CLOSEST EXIT
MAIN ENTRANCE
P

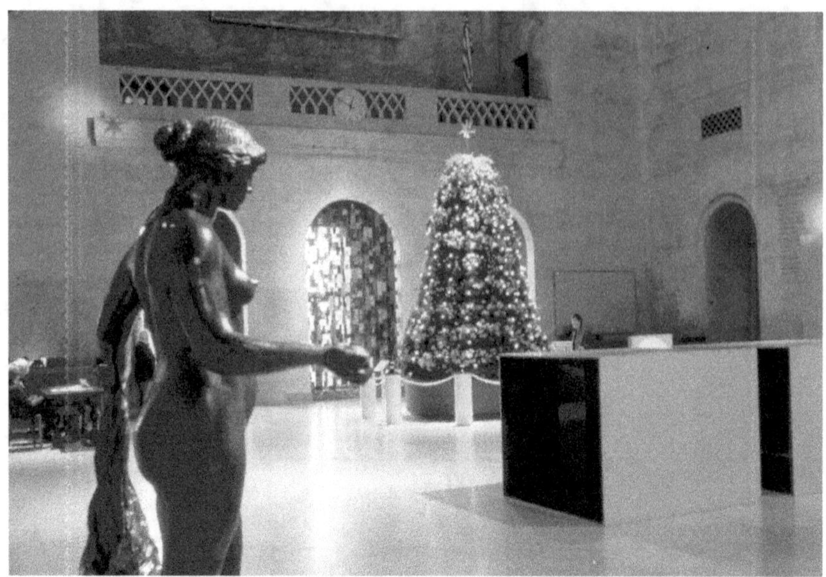

Saint Louis Art Museum, Sculpture Hall (c. 1973)
(Top) Information desk to left and guard station to right of the main entrance. (Below) The background shows a temporary partition wall covering the outside wall facing Sculpture Hall. The same type of partition wall extended Gallery 16 (a.k.a. 216) and housed Nude *before it was taken from the museum. The Picasso was estimated to be just 150 feet from the main doors.*

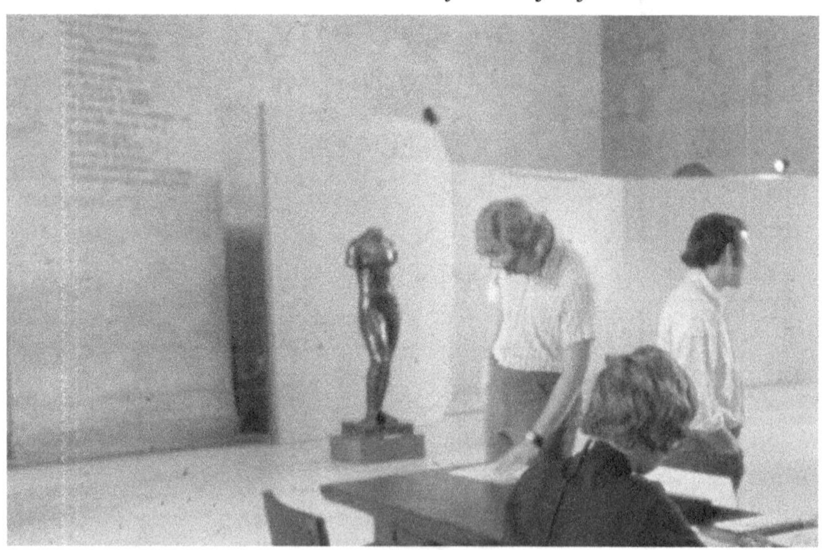

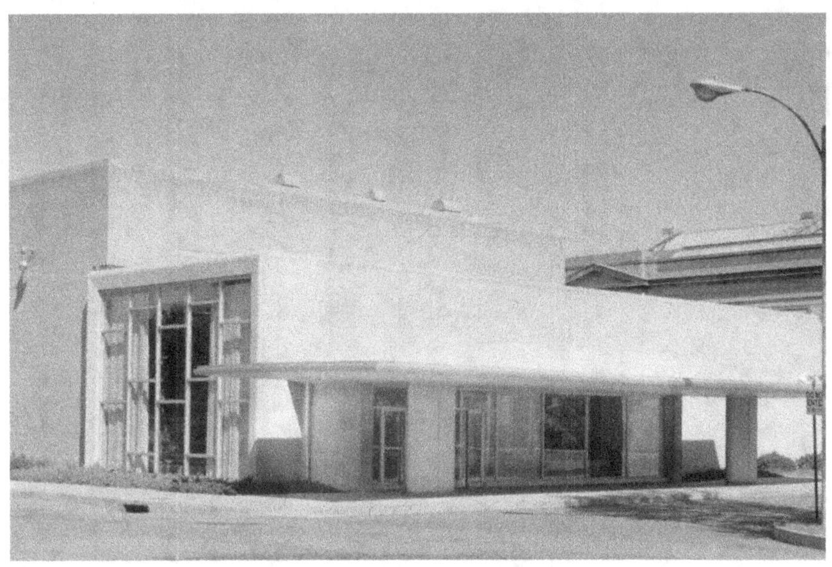

Saint Louis Art Museum, Auditorium Entrance, 1973
(Top) The second museum access point was through the auditorium lobby on the south side of the museum. (Below) Guard station at the auditorium lobby. The least convenient exit for a thief to leave the museum with Nude.

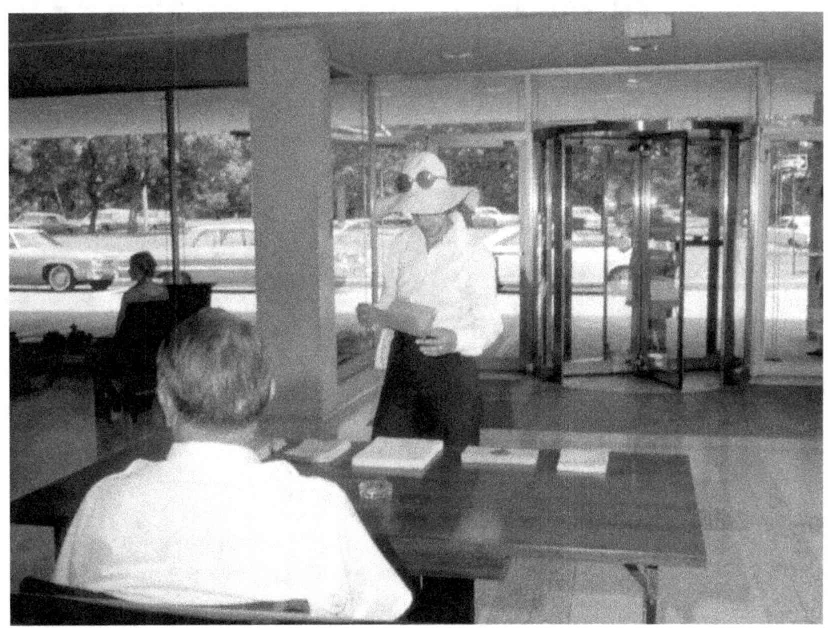

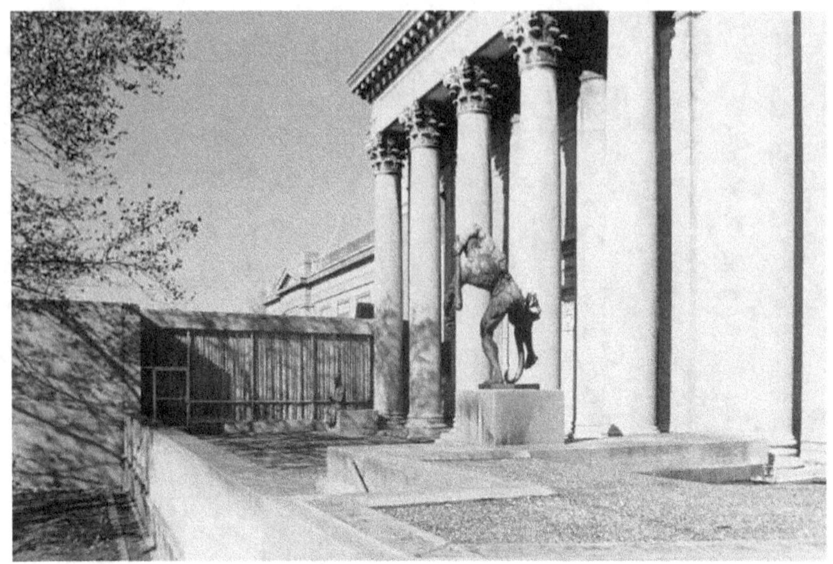

Sculpture Terrace & Auditorium Lobby Doors
(Top) In 1973, one door from Sculpture Hall entered the terrace, though climbing the wall would not have been a subtle exit route for a daytime thief. (Bottom) During the 1978 robberies, the auditorium lobby and terrace were under construction (1977 to 1980) when thieves entered the east wing.

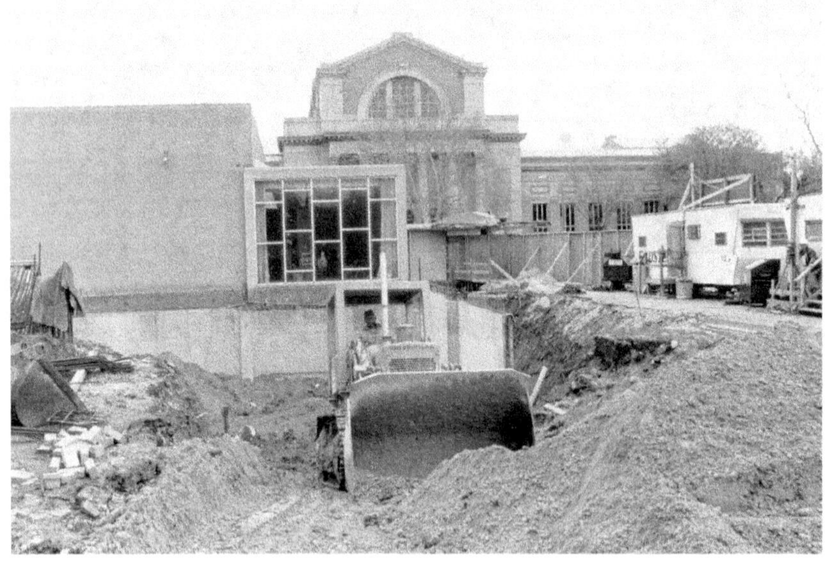

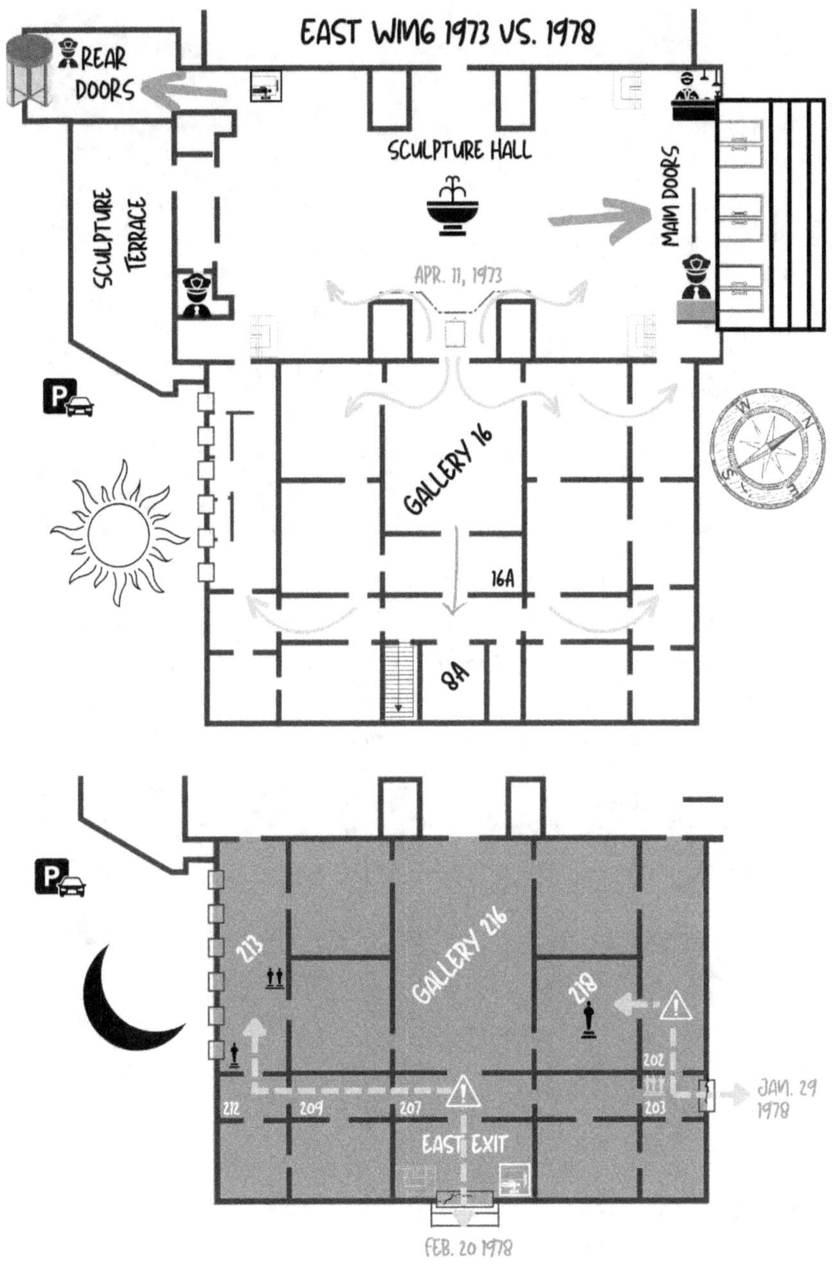
EAST WING 1973 VS. 1978
REAR DOORS
SCULPTURE TERRACE
SCULPTURE HALL
MAIN DOORS
APR. 11, 1973
GALLERY 16
16A
8A
GALLERY 216
213
218
202
203
212
209
207
EAST EXIT
JAN. 29 1978
FEB. 20 1978

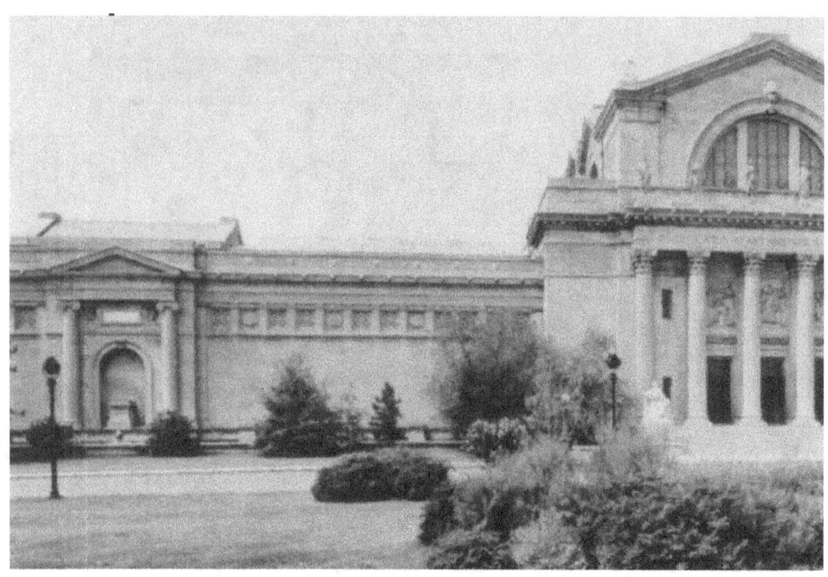

Saint Louis Art Museum, East Wing Façade
(Top) In 1973, a cement alcove with a pedestal was still featured on the east wing's north façade. (Bottom left) The 1977 renovation replaced the alcove with a glass window. Thieves broke the glass on January 29, 1978 and stole the Remington bronze from Gallery 218.

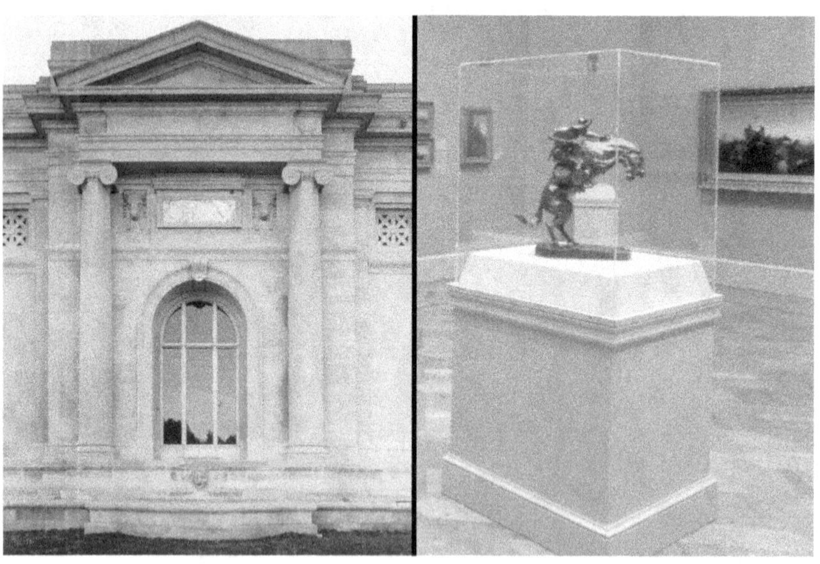

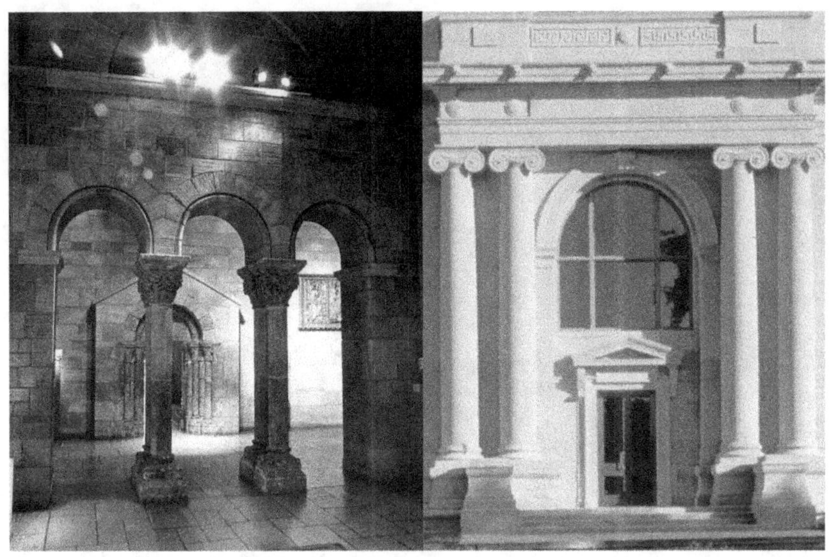

Saint Louis Art Museum, East Wing
(Left) In 1973, the Medieval Gallery (8A) blocked the east exit door.
(Right) In 1978, the door was reestablished as an exit.
A thief broke the door's glass panel, entered the museum,
and stole three Rodin statues in just sixty seconds.
(Bottom) Gallery 213 and how it would have looked the night of the robbery.
Security was unaware of the missing Rodins until the following day.
The door in view was the thief's entry point into the gallery.

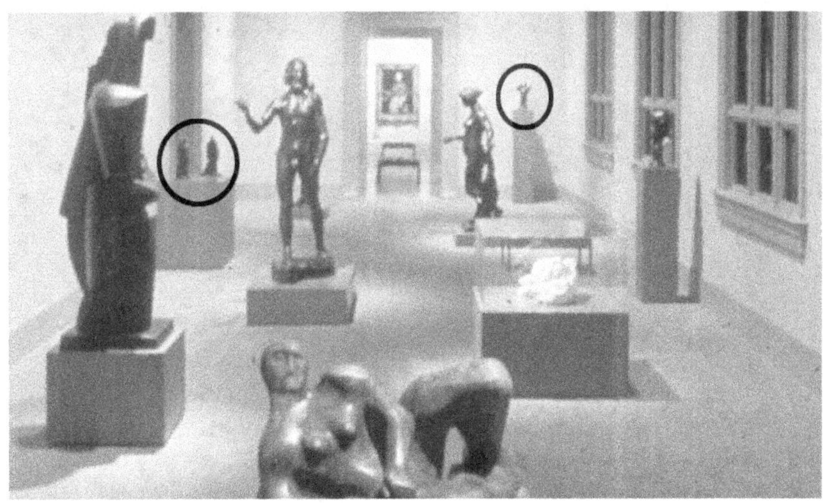

Where Art Thou, Picasso?

THE GOLDEN ANNIVERSARY of Picasso's death seemed to be the perfect time to rekindle the story of the lost painting from the Saint Louis Art Museum. Art galleries and museums worldwide might take the opportunity to formally acknowledge the master with exhibits of his life and works. It would also be fitting that *Nude* come out of hiding: resurrected from the depths of a basement, removed from the cold storage of a free port shell company, or just acknowledged as hanging in someone's home.

Though I had a good idea how *Nude* disappeared, I had no idea where it was or the condition it was in after fifty years. Narrowing the location down geographically or having some new clues in the case could breathe life into the search for *Nude*. With no case records for old clues and the historical research coming to a close, I decided on something less conventional to locate *Nude*: psychic spies.

Stanford Research Institute scientists started the Remote Viewing (RV) program around the early 1970s.[1] The research led to government-funded psychic spy programs in the military and intelligence agencies for nearly thirty years. Essentially, the program used psychic impressions to remotely view targets, often to spy on enemy activities during the Cold War.

A viewer, with no knowledge of the target, followed a proven protocol to receive impressions about a undisclosed location. They would psychically tap into the unknown target, then write and draw information to describe the location as they received it. In some cases, viewers received impressions of locations as they looked in the past, suggesting the experience might be accessing some other etheric realm.

At this point, it could not hurt to find potential new clues about the painting, where it could be, and who might have been involved in the crime. I was also curious to know if the viewers might hit on some of the information I had found through historical research. Was the painting in good shape, or had it been destroyed? Would they be able to touch on any of the facts I had found? Was the theft an organized crime hit or just some lone opportunist?

Working with a local RV instructor, she gathered ten current and former students trained in the technique. Chasing Picasso, psychically, was a unique opportunity for the students to practice RV. The remote viewers only knew they were looking for a piece of missing art. They did not know anything about the art, when or where it disappeared, or the theories behind the theft until after the session.

The students worked independently so they were not feeding each other ideas in the raw results. However, students were not experienced enough to typically separate tuned-in results from those created in the mind. Individually, it would be difficult to discern an actual RV hit in the case of stolen art. But with a group, repeated hits might point to an actual clue about the theft and the stolen painting's whereabouts.

The theft was so long ago it was unlikely the remote viewers had knowledge of the 1973 art robbery. However, personal beliefs and perceptions of art and art thefts (such as the *Dr. No* theory) could affect the results.

After a short meditation, the students were given a code assigned to the target, but never given an image or details about the stolen art. The students began drawing their first impressions. In an RV session, the first results were considered raw. During the raw session, several one-off descriptions including locations, landmarks, and people were mentioned, but some were too generic to consider valid.

However, there were a couple unique hits worth mentioning. Two viewers both hit on two different popular figures from the same era (1960s–1970s), and both having the same first names: Jimmy/James. With some interpretation, the name also resonated with the research.

Viewer 1: Jimmy Hoffa. The powerful union leader had direct ties to St. Louis mob attorney Morris Shenker. But Hoffa also lived in Detroit and had a direct relationship with members of the Detroit Mafia. St. Louis and the Detroit Mafia also worked together. The Remington that was stolen in 1978 was allegedly sent to Detroit before it was returned to St. Louis and recovered. Perhaps the random reference meant *Nude's* disappearance was on similar orders from the Mafia.

Viewer 2: James Bond. With regards to art, the first Bond movie, *Dr. No*, became the basis for the Dr. No theory. The viewer could be associating the crime with the perception of a wealthy villain. Bond could also represent just a spy, implying an inside job. Or perhaps it was just a simple impression to get the viewer to identify with the first name James.

Forty percent of the viewers mentioned Italy in the raw results, while the rest each mentioned a different country or region. Half the viewers connected to loss, grief, or sadness (Picasso dying three days before *Nude* was stolen is a possible explanation for the connection.)

Five viewers reported the art was wrapped, covered, or enclosed and put away in a storage room, like a basement, attic, or beneath the stairs. Four identified the building as being part of or close to small shops (bakery, coffee, et cetera). Three mentioned the smell of tobacco.

After the raw data, the instructor guided the group through a series of questions. The purpose was to gather immediate impressions about the whereabouts and perpetrators of the crime using some general prompts to illicit a more detailed response.

The majority believed the theft was an inside job; however, they were evenly divided across their choices (i.e., director, curator, archivist, restoration, et cetera), rendering them unreliable. Security was not a choice, but one viewer verbally named the position as the insider role. Another said a staff member looked away, and a third mentioned an outsider disguised as a member.

Knowing the circumstances of the theft, the last three seemed reasonable responses. The RV group did not know: 1) the theft was reported forty-two hours after it happened, 2) the painting was displayed about 150 feet from the exit door guarded by security, 3) the gallery had a dedicated security guard in Gallery 16, and 4) the last person to report seeing it was a security guard.

The prompted choices also contradicted the raw data; 66 percent of the viewers chose Europe when asked about location, but just 40 percent in the raw data gave specific countries in Europe. And 10 percent chose North America, but 40 percent cited locations in North America in the raw data. Half the group chose an art ring as being behind the theft, and 30 percent chose an individual. However, everyone agreed the art was not destroyed and that it will be recovered. And if I were to believe the results of the session, then *Nude* has lived a sheltered life in storage. If true, it was a fitting scenario for the obscure painting, which had dodged art catalogs and databases for over a century.

UNLUCKY NUDE

A string of bad luck seemed to follow Amélie Lang from the time she was born out of wedlock in Paris, 1881. In her memoirs, she recalled having a loveless childhood. Her mom abandoned her, allegedly for being an unruly child. She lived in Paris with an aunt and uncle, to their dismay. They forced her into marriage at eighteen to a man who raped and beat her. At nineteen years old, she escaped her abusive husband, changed her name to Fernande Olivier, and began a career as an artist's model. She worked at Montmartre, a neighborhood in north Paris where many great artists called home, including a young prodigy who had recently shortened his name to Picasso.[2]

Picasso painted, sketched, and sculpted numerous pieces of art that featured the model, Olivier, though most were produced once she became his live-in mistress in 1905. Since she was technically still married to her first husband, she could never legally marry Picasso. Olivier was with Picasso for about seven years, and most of the time, they struggled financially, barely able to buy food. Shortly after Picasso painted *Nude*, there must have been some financial improvement, as they adopted a thirteen-year-old child in 1907, even though they ended up giving her back to the orphanage just four months later. Just as Picasso was starting to make a name for himself, the couple broke up in 1911. Olivier lived through the struggles of the young artist but would not live the grand lifestyle that Picasso eventually achieved from his art.

Nude ironically reflected aspects of Olivier's life, not just her image. A troubled past was followed by bad timing. Olivier died a year before *Nude* finally made it into a Picasso Rose Period catalog, and it was full of art she inspired. Then, six years later, *Nude* was stolen from the art museum. Perhaps when Picasso captured the essence of Olivier on the wooden canvas, it included her bad luck.

The art museum deaccessioned *Nude* sometime after receiving the disappointing insurance payment that shorted the value by more than 50 percent. The theft of *La Tante Marie* led to the discovery of a second painting on the reverse side of the canvas and increased her value. The underinsured Picasso suffered the polar opposite fate. Should *Nude* have a secret painting of "Clothed" on its backside, we may never know.

Given the length of its disappearance, it could mean the painting might be put up for sale soon. The painting could be worth millions of dollars with the right auction house. Legitimate art dealers and auction houses must reference stolen art lists before a transaction to minimize their own risks. Would they find *Nude* on the NSAF? No. How about the Art Loss Register? Not sure since they wouldn't respond to my inquiries. When *Nude* was stolen, it was reported to the Art Dealers Association of America and added to their list of stolen art in 1973. Hopefully, that list survived the decades.

The FBI's stolen database effectively brought *Russian School Children* to the attention of Spielberg's assistant, even though the painting resurfaced in 1988 and was no longer stolen. Maybe someone on the FBI art recovery team will be so kind as to finally list the other painting taken in St. Louis in 1973 that is still missing. And please, use all of its known titles: *Kneeling Nude Arranging Her Hair, A Study in Nude, Study for Kneeling Woman Combing Her Hair, Kneeling Nude Combing Her Hair, Etude pour Femme Agenouillée se Coiffant, Nu agenouillé se coiffant,* and not just the generic, forgetful *Nude.* (Though I appreciate the brevity of *Nude* for the book.)

Raising awareness of the Picasso art theft was the best opportunity to get *Study for Kneeling Woman Combing Her Hair* (and its many English and French titles) on multiple stolen art databases. This would allow almost anyone to quickly identify it as stolen art. And just maybe we can change *Nude's* luck.

Social media and the internet could breathe new life into this cold case simply by spreading the word about a piece of stolen art. The modern communication platforms reach millions worldwide, increasing the opportunity for art recovery where there has previously been none—an advantage the missing Picasso from the St. Louis museum did not have in 1973.

SEARCHING FOR NUDE

The surrounding events in 1973 provided some hope *Nude* was still inside the country, just as the Rockwell resurfaced in New Orleans. The Remington allegedly made a pit stop in Detroit before returning to the art museum, another sign the painting could still be in domestic territory.

Why should anyone care about a piece of art or bother to search for it? The question popped into my mind repeatedly when writing about the forgotten story of *Nude*. However, I learned about the stolen Picasso when I was on a different treasure hunt involving a significantly less expensive piece of art. The best part about the hunt was the adventure. I realized that searching for the missing Picasso was similar and practically anyone could participate.

Leave the dangerous work to recover art on the black market with the professionals and chase the Picasso at a safe distance. A real-life *Where's Waldo?* adventure was what I had in mind. Instead of looking for a narrow-faced teen wearing glasses, jeans, and a striped red-and-white sweater and matching hat, people can look for the small black-and-white oil painting about the size of a sheet of legal paper.

Nude could be hiding anywhere. Sift through the piles of junk in the attic, basement, or storage room. Go to an antique store and peek at the old paintings for sale. Look at the art hanging on the walls in local restaurants and watering holes.

Don't be afraid to visit an estate sale. That eccentric neighbor with an artsy flair or squirrelly demeanor may have lifted a Picasso in their prime and left a valuable painting among a houseful of old *Life* magazines.

Tour those quaint stores and historic buildings with the purpose of the chase and watch it turn a boring adventure through an antique aisle into something a little more exciting. Fascinating histories, interesting characters, and hidden neighborhood gems like parks, diners, and shops await the searcher willing to chase *Nude*.

Lastly, an armchair hunt has its merits too. I spent time during a few COVID-19 quarantines and while healing a broken foot searching online auction houses and eBay. I suspect *Nude* could be coming up for sale if the demand for Picasso art resurges during the fiftieth anniversary year of his death. And just maybe someone who reads the story of the missing Picasso will be lucky enough to spot it.

I FOUND THE PICASSO IN MY ATTIC. NOW WHAT?

Despite the unfamiliarity of *Nude*, Picasso boldly painted his signature across the top of the painting, which was this piece of art's most recognizable feature. As long as no one has gone to the extent of hiding his mark, finding *Nude* might not be as difficult as it seems.

If the reader suddenly discovered they had the painting in their possession, could they keep it? The short answer: seek a lawyer for advice before putting it up for sale.

Finding the art (as opposed to a good-faith purchase) would default to the owner. In this case, it would likely be the Saint Louis Art Museum, assuming the insurance company did not have a claim for the title. In most cases, the claimant (gallery/museum) would return the initial payment they received to the insurance company and regain title to the painting.

Restitution cases have unique circumstances; therefore, different laws apply to stolen art looted in WWII. This would not apply to *Nude.* However, Article 2 of The Uniform Commercial Code (UCC), a collection of laws adopted in every state, applies to stolen art like *Nude.*

Under this law, the seller of stolen art does not possess a good title. Therefore, title cannot be transferred to a buyer. Not even a good-faith purchaser can obtain title, regardless of where they purchased it…auction, private sale, or subsequent buyer who purchased from a thief.[3]

If the art turns out to be located in another country, then foreign property laws could apply. Italy completely supports good-faith purchase transactions. In France, the original owner must reimburse the good-faith purchaser to get the art back.[4] As much art as criminals have stolen from Italy and France, it was surprising to learn they protect good-faith purchases of stolen art. The bad news, of course, was that if *Nude* had made its way overseas, the painting would not likely return to the museum's hands without a miracle.

Nude came from the city's art museum (not a federal institution). Since the painting held a value over $5,000, it would be a federal offense *if* the art crossed state lines in 1973. (Today, museum thefts are always a federal crime, even if the goods do not cross a state line.) The current statute of limitations for the federal crime of stealing art from a museum has been raised to twenty-five years, though *Nude* has been gone double that amount.

If the art stayed within Missouri and state law applied to the case, the theft would have been a Class C felony. The statute of limitations was three years. I doubt any court could prosecute such an old case as the FBI and police files for the crime were destroyed. After fifty years, no one could actually prove who stole *Nude.*

On the slim chance the thief, or the thief's relative, is reading this book and has the painting, please seek advice from a criminal defense attorney before telling the world *Nude* has been hanging in the guest bathroom for the last half-century.

Essentially, a person finding, inheriting, or purchasing stolen art in good faith in the United States can never rightfully own *Study for Kneeling Woman Combing Her Hair.* It belongs to the Saint Louis Art Museum, one of the few places to view centuries' worth of stunning art for free.

Since the painting remained in hiding all these years, maybe whoever has it can kindly send it back, gift-wrapped with a big bow and a fiftieth-anniversary card, to the museum in April 2023. I can't imagine a better ending than having it returned to the Saint Louis Art Museum. Although capturing the storied return in a revised version of this book, aptly named *Finding Picasso,* would be a close second.

MISSING

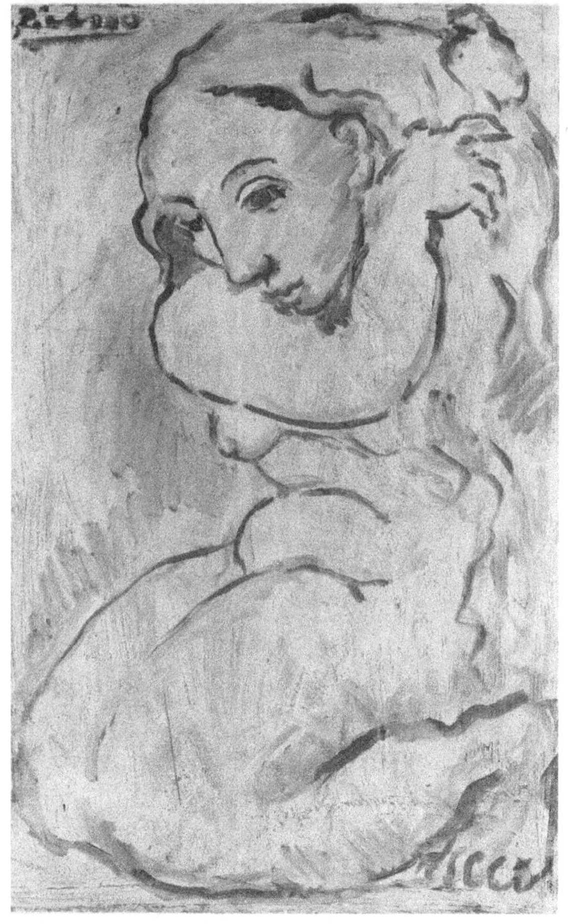

Last Seen: *April 11, 1973*
Etude pour Femme Agenouillée se Coiffant, (1906)
Study for Kneeling Woman Combing Her Hair *or* Nude
By Pablo Picasso, Spanish, 1881-1973
(Oil on Wood, 8½ × 14 $^{1}\!/_{16}$ inches)
©2023 Estate of Pablo Picasso / Artists Rights Society (ARS), New York
If you have seen this painting, submit a lead at cjoanbaker.com.

ACKNOWLEDGMENTS

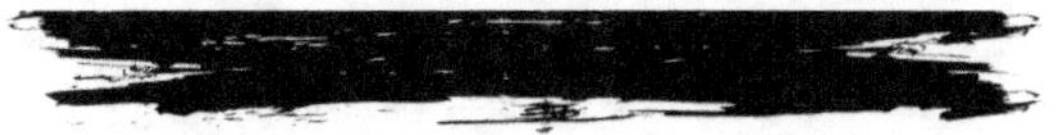

A big thanks to the greatest fan, and spouse, Rod, who supported my decision to leave behind a secure paycheck for a chance to write books. You fed me and kept me hydrated as I became oblivious to time. Cheers to another thirty-plus years of memories together!

The book would not be possible without the investigators, journalists, and reporters who recorded local history and reported on the art thefts. Without them, the story of the missing Picasso from the museum would be completely dead. Additionally, the backstory of the painting would not have been possible without the knowledgeable, courteous staff of the Saint Louis Art Museum. They were kind enough to look into the dusty archives to help uncover a critical clue in the painting's history.

I want to acknowledge all who answered phone calls and emails from this stranger looking for leads in the story. Thanks for taking the call and sparing a few minutes to chat or promptly reply to my emails. A special thanks to retired FBI Agent and art theft expert Robert K. Wittman for kindly accepting the invitation to read and comment on the book in advance.

The book's final form would not exist without the help of talented editors and a couple of avid readers willing to provide feedback. Thanks to Lori L. for bravely reading my first unedited manuscript. Likewise, thank you, Tom I., for reading the manuscript in between the final edits. A BIG thanks to Andrew Doty and the Editwright team for their professional edits, insight, and fantastic direction.

Thanks to the loving support of so many: my children, Kyle and Madison; my sisters, Pat, Chris, Linda, and the GWE niece crew; Kramer, the mini Aussie who took ME on walks when I needed a break from the keyboard; and my gal pals who have spent almost two golf seasons hearing about this story.

Lastly, thanks to all the strangers I met who showed interest in the story after asking what I was writing about and continued to listen. They did not pretend to take a fake phone call to get away from me. I took it as a good sign.

NOTES

Chapter 1. The Passing of Two Picassos

1   "Museum Gets Bargain through Shifts in Taste," *St. Louis Post-Dispatch*, June 18, 1965.

2   Charlene Bry, "Art Museum Bad Day Still Vivid: The Day A Picasso Was Stolen," *St. Louis Globe-Democrat*, June 28, 1973.

3   John Brod Peters, "Intensive Search On for Museum's Stolen Picasso," *St. Louis Globe-Democrat*, April 17, 1973.

4   Bry, "Bad Day."

5   Bry, "Bad Day."

6   Bry, "Bad Day."

7   John Barelli and Zachary Schisgal, "Be My Valentine," in *Stealing the Show: A History of Art and Crime in Six Thefts* (Guilford, CT: The Lyons Press, 2019), 7.

8   Barelli and Schisgal, "My Valentine," 9–13.

9   United Press International, "IRA Boss Suspected in Art Heist," *The Morning Herald*, Maryland, May 6, 1974, https://www.newspapers.com/image/28279563.

10 George McCue, "Museum's Role Conflicts with Security," *St. Louis Post-Dispatch*, April 15, 1973.

11 Charles Furvis, "Why the Outbreak of International Art Thefts?" *St. Louis Globe-Democrat*, August 28, 1961.

12 Associated Press, "Cultural Crime: Rising Tide of Art Thefts," *St. Louis Post-Dispatch*, January 16, 1969.

13 Donald L. Mason, *The Fine Art of Art Security: Protecting Public and Private Collections against Theft, Fire and Vandalism* (New York: Van Nostrand, 1979), 5.

14 "Matisse Painting Expected to Rise $50,000 Value," *The St. Louis Star and Times*, December 5, 1945.

15 "Cezanne Acquired by Art Museum," *St. Louis Post-Dispatch*, August 29, 1934.

Chapter 2. Degenerate Art

1   Associated Press, "Organized Crime Dips into Art Thievery," *Wisconsin State Journal*, March 20, 1977, https://www.newspapers.com/image/401103577.

2   John Launius, *The Life and Times of Missouri's Charles Parsons: Between Art and War* (Charleston: The History Press, 2020), 91.

3   Noah Charney, "Looting," in *The Museum of Lost Art* (New York: Phaidon Press Inc., 2018), 51.

4   Simon Houpt, "Art as a Commodity," in *Museum of the Missing: A History of Art Theft* (New York: Sterling Pub., 2006), 33–34.

5   Benjamin Blake Evemy, "Great Art Heists of History: The Nazis' War Against Modern Art," *Mutual Art,* https://www.mutualart.com/Article/Great-Art-Heists-of-History--The-Nazis-W/B032DD496FA92EFD#.

6   Henri Matisse, *Bathers with a Turtle*, 1908, oil on canvas, 71½" × 87", Saint Louis Art Museum, https://www.slam.org/collection/objects/5335.

7   Hulton v. The Free State of Bavaria, No. 16-cv-9360 (US New York, December 5, 2016).

8   Nancy Kenney, "Guggenheim to Return Kirchner Painting to Heirs of Jewish Dealer," *The Art Newspaper,* https://www.theartnewspaper.com/2018/10/04/guggenheim-to-return-kirchner-painting-to-heirs-of-jewish-dealer.

9   Ernst Ludwig Kirchner, *View from the Window*, 1914, oil on canvas, 47½" × 35¾", Saint Louis Art Museum, https://www.slam.org/collection/objects/13494.

10   Karl Schmidt-Rottluff, *Village on the Sea*, 1913, oil on canvas, 30¼" × 35¾", Saint Louis Art Museum, https://www.slam.org/collection/objects/13536.

11   Evemy, "Great Art Heists."

12   Max Beckmann, *Christ and the Sinner,* 1917, oil on canvas, 58¾" × 49⅞", Saint Louis Art Museum, https://www.slam.org/collection/objects/1462.

13   Fred Abrams, "Mr. Curt Valentin's Nazi-Looted Art: Hidden Money Search," *Asset Search Blog,* October 24, 2017, https://www.assetsearchblog.com/2008/11/09/mr-curt-valentins-nazi-looted-art.

14   "Archives Directory for the History of Collecting," *The Frick Collection* (New York) February 7, 2020, https://research.frick.org/directory/detail/99.

15 Perry T. Rathbone, "A Tribute to Curt Valentin: An Exhibition of Twentieth Century Art Selected from St. Louis Collections," *Bulletin of the City Art Museum of St. Louis* 39, no. 2/3 (February 1955), 1–20, http://www.jstor.org/stable/40715188.

16 "Two Expressionist Masterworks Restituted to the Heirs of Collector, Dealer and Bon Vivant Alfred Flechtheim," *Sotheby's* (October 29, 2018), https://www.sothebys.com/en/articles/two-expressionist-masterworks-restituted-to-the-heirs-of-collector-dealer-and-bon-vivant-alfred-flechtheim.

17 Charles Dellheim, "Chapter 18. Artless Jews," in *Belonging and Betrayal: How Jews Made the Art World Modern* (Waltham, MA: Brandeis University Press, 2021), 435–439.

18 William D. Cohan, "MoMA's Problematic Provenances," *ARTnews* (November 18, 2019), https://www.artnews.com/art-news/news/momas-problematic-provenances-477.

19 "Art Dealer of the Avante-Garde: Artists," *Alfred Flechtheim,* http://alfredflechtheim.com/en/artists.

20 Hulton v. The Free State of Bavaria, No. 16-cv-9360 (US New York, Dec. 05, 2016).

21 Cohan, "Problematic Provenances."

Chapter 3. Swindled Art

1 Fernande Olivier, "In Love with Picasso: Fernande's Journal, Fall 1906–March 1907," in *Loving Picasso: The Private Journal of Fernande Olivier* (New York: Harry N. Abrams, 2001), 161–188.

2 Olivier, "In Love," 161–188.

3 John Richardson and Marilyn McCully, "L'Affaire Picasso," in *A Life of Picasso* (New York: Alfred A. Knopf, 2007), 410.

4 Richardson and McCully, "L'Affaire," 403.

5 Richardson and McCully, "L'Affaire," 404.

6 Richardson and McCully, "L'Affaire," 405.

7 Laurence Madeline, "Picasso and the Calvet Affair of 1930," *The Burlington Magazine,* 147, no. 1226 (May 2005): 316, http://www.jstor.org/stable/20073963.

8 Richardson and McCully, "L'Affaire," 404.

9   Madeline, "Calvet Affair," 318.

10   Richardson and McCully, "L'Affaire," 404.

11   Richardson and McCully, "L'Affaire," 406.

12   "Eugène Zak," *Bureau d'art Ecole de Paris*, March 8, 2022, http://ecoledeparis.org/eugene-zak.

13   Madeline, "Calvet Affair," 318.

14   Richardson and McCully, "L'Affaire," 410.

15   "Museum Gets Bargain through Shifts in Taste," *St. Louis Post-Dispatch*, June 18, 1965.

Chapter 4. The Enigma of Art Value

1   "What Makes Art Valuable?" *SamsOriginalArt*, June 22, 2019, https://samsoriginalart.com/what-makes-art-valuable.

2   Pablo Picasso, *Picasso: The Blue and Rose Periods,* edited by Raphael Bouvier, Riehn, Switzerland, The Foundation Beyeler, 2019.

3   "Art Valuable?" SamsOriginalArt.

4   "Art Valuable?" SamsOriginalArt.

5   "What Makes Art Valuable?" *The Collector,* November 15, 2021, https://www.thecollector.com/what-makes-art-valuable.

6   John Richardson and Marilyn McCully, "L'Affaire Picasso," in *A Life of Picasso* (New York: Alfred A. Knopf, 2007), 406.

7   "Ambroise Vollard Patron of the Avante Garde," *Chicago Art Institute,* October 12, 2008, http://www.artic.edu/aic/exhibitions/picasso/themes.html.

8   "The 'Cubists' Dominate Paris' Fall Salon," *New York Times,* October 8, 1911.

9   *Portrait of a Young Man,* 1662, oil on canvas, 35⅜" × 27⅞", Saint Louis Art Museum, March 31, 2022, https://www.slam.org/collection/objects/38157.

10   Oscar Holland, "Pennsylvania Museum's Disputed Portrait Is a Rembrandt, Research Says," *Cable News Network (CNN),* February 18, 2020, https://www.cnn.com/style/article/rembrandt-allentown-pennsylvania-portrait/index.html.

11   Denise Blostein, Robert Libetti, and Kelly Crow, "How a $450 Million Da Vinci Was Lost in America—and Later Found," *The Wall Street Journal,* September 19, 2018, https://www.wsj.com/articles/fresh-details-reveal-how-450-million-da-vinci-was-lost-in-americaand-later-found-1537305592.

12   *Savior for Sale,* directed by Antoine Vitkine (Greenwich Entertainment, 2021), Amazon Prime Video, https://www.amazon.com/gp/video/detail/B09GHLCF2Y.

13   *The Lost Leonardo,* directed by Andreas Koefoed (Sony Pictures Classics, 2021), Amazon Prime Video, https://www.amazon.com/gp/video/detail/B09LHCS76S.

14   Koefoed, *The Lost Leonardo.*

15   Koefoed, *The Lost Leonardo.*

16   Shirley M. Mueller, "The Collector's Decision," in *Inside the Head of a Collector: Neuropsychological Forces at Play* (Seattle: Lucia/Marquand, 2019), 94–97.

17   Mueller, "Collector's Decision," 97.

18   Simon Houpt, "Art as a Commodity," in *Museum of the Missing: A History of Art Theft* (New York: Sterling Pub., 2006), 16.

Chapter 5. A French Secret on Art Hill

1   "Louis IX Now a Disarmingly Easy Rider on Art Hill," *St. Louis Post-Dispatch,* December 9, 1981.

2   Caroline Loughlin and Catherine Anderson, "Appendix 1. Buildings, Statues, and Monuments," in *Forest Park* (Columbia, MO: Univ. of Missouri Press, 1986), 260.

3   "Niehaus Will Accept $3000," *St. Louis Post-Dispatch* 1879–1922, May 21, 1907, https://www.proquest.com/historical-newspapers/druggisis-have-no-fear-federal-court-ruling/docview/579830526/se-2.

4   "A $7500 Piece of Art," *St. Louis-Globe Democrat,* August 30, 1934.

5   "4 Art Thieves Go to Prison," *Corpus Christi Times* (Texas), December 23, 1961.

6   "8 Stolen Paintings Recovered: City Art Museum's Included," *St. Louis Post-Dispatch,* April 11, 1962.

7   "2 Million in Paintings Stolen," *Battle Creek Inquirer* (Michigan), July 17, 1961.

8   Associated Press, "Stolen Cézannes Recovered," *Press and Sun-Bulletin* (Binghamton, NY), April 11, 1962.

9   "Stolen Cézannes."

10   Charles, Furvis, "Why the Outbreak of International Art Thefts?" *St. Louis Globe-Democrat,* August 28, 1961.

11   "Reward Offer for Stolen Cezanne Masterpieces," *St. Louis Post-Dispatch,* August 27, 1961.

12   Sylvia Porter, "Art Masterpiece Thefts Becoming Common Place," *Ft. Worth Telegram* (Texas), August 21, 1961.

13   Porter, "Art Masterpiece."

14   "Art Proves Blessing in Disguise," *St. Louis Globe-Democrat,* September 5, 1962.

15   "St. Louis Cezanne That Was Stolen Has Another Picture on the Back," *St. Louis Post-Dispatch,* September 4, 1962.

16   Associated Press, "Cultural Crime: Rising Tide of Art Thefts," *St. Louis Post-Dispatch,* January 16, 1969.

Chapter 6. The Art of Organized Crime

1   Associated Press, "Cultural Crime: Rising Tide of Art Thefts," *St. Louis Post-Dispatch,* January 16, 1969.

2   Noah Charney, "What's the Motive Behind Most Art Thefts? These Mafia Heists Provide Clues," *Observer,* July 9, 2018, https://observer.com/2018/07/mafia-heists-provide-clues-to-motive-behind-famous-art-thefts.

3   "War on Organized Crime Faltering—Federal Strike Forces Not Getting the Job Done," *Department of Justice* (Washington, DC: US Accounting Office, March 1977), 1–7, https://www.gao.gov/assets/ggd-77-117.

4   DOJ, "Crime Faltering."

5   DOJ, "Crime Faltering."

6   Associated Press, "International Thefts of Art Link to Drugs and Politics," *The Philadelphia Inquirer,* September 12, 1976.

7   Ted Gest, "Anti-crime Agency Sought: State Unit Proposed in Fight on Crime," *St. Louis-Post Dispatch*, January 6, 1971.

8   C.D. Stelzer, "Art Berne: A Shot in the Dark," *STL Reporter*, February 5, 2015, https://stlreporter.com/2015/02/15/a-shot-in-the-dark/.

9   Scott Burnstein, "Mafia Hit List—Top St. Louis Mob Murders," *Gangster Report*, July 16, 2014, https://gangsterreport.com/the-hit-list-st-louis.

10   Theodore C. Link, "Parlay Cards Appear Despite Raid on Plant," *St. Louis-Post Dispatch*, November 29, 1969.

11   "Organized Crime and Use of Violence, Hearings, Part 2" (Washington, DC: US Congress, May 1980), 400–406, https://www.ojp.gov/pdffiles1/Digitization/72649NCJRS.pdf.

12   "Assembly to Get Anticrime Plan," *St. Louis Post-Dispatch*, January 6, 1971.

13   Denny Walsh, "The Mayor, the Mob and the Lawyer," *Life Magazine*, May 29, 1970, 24–31.

14   Edward H. Thorton, "Shenker Fee in Sale: $500,000," *St. Louis Post-Dispatch*, January 6, 1971.

15   Theodore C. Link, "Las Vegas Junkets Backed By 2 Here," *St. Louis Post-Dispatch*, June 11, 1972.

16   Al Delugach, "Reputed Mob Figures Hosted by Vegas Hotel: Free Rooms, Meals and Liquor Given to 20 Men with Alleged Links to Organized Crime," *Los Angeles Times*, December 15, 1974.

17   Ronald J. Lawrence, "U.S. Inquiry into State Pardons," *St. Louis Post-Dispatch*, October 28, 1973.

18   Edward H. Thornton, "Links Emprise Firm to Hoodlums," *St. Louis Post-Dispatch*, April 16, 1972.

19   Ronald J. Lawrence and Roy Malone, "Anthony Giordano: When He Spoke, Mob Listened," *St. Louis Post-Dispatch*, August 31, 1980.

20   Lawrence, "Anthony Giordano."

Chapter 7. The Art of Fencing

1   "Norman Rockwell: A Brief Biography," *Norman Rockwell Museum*, April 5, 2021, https://www.nrm.org/about/about-2/about-norman-rockwell.

2   "$20,000 Rockwell Oil Painting Stolen from Gallery in Clayton," *St. Louis Globe-Democrat*, June 26, 1973.

3   "Rockwell Work Is Stolen from Clayton Shop," *St. Louis Post-Dispatch*, June 26, 1973.

4   Chad Garrison, "The Rockwell Files," *Riverfront Times*, June 6, 2007, https://www.riverfronttimes.com/stlouis/the-rockwell-files/Content?oid=2483090.

5   Garrison, "Rockwell Files."

6   John B. McPhee, C. Thomas Spitzer, and Robert P. Sundin, "The National Stolen Art File," in *FBI Law Enforcement Bulletin* (March 1983), 16–23, https://www.ojp.gov/pdffiles1/Digitization/88517-88521NCJRS.pdf.

7   Susan Stamberg, "Spielberg, Lucas Celebrate Rockwell's Iconic America," *NPR*, July 9, 2010, https://www.npr.org/ templates/story/story.php?storyId=128360139#.

8   Nick Divito, "Tangled Tale of a Norman Rockwell Painting," *Courthouse News Service*, May 31, 2012, https://www.courthousenews.com/tangled-tale-of-a-norman-rockwell-painting.

9   Divito, "Tangled."

10   Solomon v. Cutler, No. 2:07-cv-645-RLH-PAL (UNev, April 8, 2010), *Scribd*, https://www.scribd.com/doc/29807813/Solomon-vs-Cutler.

11   Solomon v. Cutler.

12   FBI Teletype, "Subject: Theft of Norman Rockwell Painting, Russian School Room, from Arts International Limited," October 7, 1988 (FOIPA Request #1512415-000).

13   FBI, "Russian School Room."

14   Kristen Peterson, "Art Theft! Lawsuits! Spielberg!" *Las Vegas Sun*, July 5, 2008, https://lasvegassun.com/news/2008/jul/05/art-theft-lawsuits-spielberg.

15   Solomon v. Cutler.

16   "Strategies for Combatting the Criminal Receiver (Fence) of Stolen Goods," (Washington, DC: US Depart of Justice, 1976), 8–22, https://www.ojp.gov/ncjrs/virtual-library/abstracts/strategies-combatting-criminal-receiver-stolen-goods-anti-fencing.

17   "Criminal Receiver."

18   "Criminal Receiver."

19   "Criminal Receiver."

20 Edward H. Kohn, "Officer Said to Have Warned Thief of Trap," *St. Louis Post-Dispatch*, January 24, 1978.

21 "Police Deny Leak of Data on Trap for Fences," *St. Louis Post-Dispatch*, January 31, 1978.

22 George E. Curry, "Five Accused of Fencing Stolen Jade, Glassware," *St. Louis Post-Dispatch*, January 5, 1978.

Chapter 8. *The Art of the Informant*

1 "Strategies for Combatting the Criminal Receiver (Fence) of Stolen Goods," (Washington, DC: US Depart of Justice, 1976), 8–22, https://www.ojp.gov/ncjrs/virtual-library/abstracts/strategies-combatting-criminal-receiver-stolen-goods-anti-fencing.

2 "Criminal Receiver."

3 Stanton Samenow, *Inside the Criminal Mind* (PhD diss., New York: Times Books, 1984), 95–174.

4 Stanton Samenow, *Straight Talk about Criminals: Individuals with a Criminal Mind* (Phd diss., Northvale, NJ: Jason Aronson Inc., 1998), 77.

5 Theodore C. Link and John Hynes, "Antique Shop Holdup Grows to $250,000 Case," *St. Louis Post-Dispatch*, January 14, 1974.

6 Link and Hynes, "Antique Shop."

7 Link and Hynes, "Antique Shop."

8 "The Court of Proposal to Sell Stolen Jewelry," *St. Louis Post-Dispatch*, June 6, 1973.

9 "Denies He Knew Items Were Stolen," *St. Louis Post-Dispatch*, June 7, 1973.

10 "Jury Acquits Journey of Transporting Stolen Jewelry," *St. Louis Post-Dispatch*, June 8, 1973.

11 "Journey's Attorney Seeks Inquiry on News Reports," *St. Louis Post-Dispatch*, July 3, 1973.

12 "Inquiry on Role of Judge in Federal Trial of His Nephew," *St. Louis Post-Dispatch*, June 26, 1973.

13 Sally Bixby Defty, "Ex-St. Louisan Is Questioned in Art Theft," *St. Louis Post-Dispatch*, January 24, 1978.

14 "The President John F. Kennedy Assassination Records Collection," *National Archives and Records Administration (NARA)*, https://www.archives.gov/files/research/jfk/releases/docid-32989737.pdf, 19.

15 "Busts of Lindbergh Are Stolen," *St. Louis Post-Dispatch,* January 5, 1974.

16 "Assassination Records," 4.

17 "Assassination Records," 7.

18 "Investigation of the Assassination of Martin Luther King, Jr." vol. 7 (Washington, DC: US Government 1979), 209–210, https://books.google.com/books?id=SW-z6uUxyd8C&pg.

19 "Assassination Records," 7–8.

20 "Assassination Records," 5.

21 "Assassination Records," 5.

22 "Assassination Records," 4.

23 "Assassination Records," 5.

24 "Assassination Records," 4.

25 "Assassination Records," 6.

Chapter 9. The Art of Theft & Conspiracy

1   Robert W. Duffy and Patricia Rice, "Museum Restoration," *St. Louis Post-Dispatch,* December 4, 1977.

2   Sally Bixby Defty, "Poor Security at Art Museum Angers Police," *St. Louis Post-Dispatch,* February 22, 1978.

3   "Art Museum Broken Into, 4 Statues Stolen," *St. Louis Post-Dispatch,* January 30, 1978.

4   Robert W. Duffy, "3 Rodin Works Stolen at Museum," *St. Louis Post-Dispatch,* February 21, 1978.

5   Bill Bryan, "Art Museum Is Burglarized Again," *St. Louis Globe-Democrat,* February 22, 1978.

6   Defty, "Poor Security."

7   "Statue Recovered, Man Held," *St. Louis Post-Dispatch,* February 28, 1978.

8   "Statue Recovered."

9 "Rock Hill Man, Transient Accused in Museum Case; 1 Statue Found," *St. Louis Globe-Democrat*, March 1, 1978.

10 "The President John F. Kennedy Assassination Records Collection," *National Archives and Records Administration (NARA)*, https://www.archives.gov/files/research/jfk/releases/docid-32989737.pdf, 19.

11 S.B. Defty and J. Pulitzer, "Police Say Stolen Statue Was 'Ordered'," *St. Louis Post-Dispatch*, March 1, 1978.

12 Rich Kurre, "On the Trail of Stolen Art Objects," *St. Louis-Globe Democrat*, April 13, 1978.

13 "Two Museum Statues Recovered at Motel," *St. Louis Post-Dispatch*, March 12, 1978.

14 "Police Get Tip, Recover Stolen Museum Statue," *St. Louis Globe-Democrat*, April 8–9, 1978.

15 Kurre, "On the Trail."

16 Mary Scarpinato, "Last of Stolen Museum Sculptures Recovered," *St. Louis-Globe Democrat*, April 12, 1978.

17 Sally Bixby Defty, "Police Investigated for Arrest of Man in Art Museum Thefts," *St. Louis Post-Dispatch*, May 12, 1978.

18 Defty, "Arrest of Man."

19 Defty, "Arrest of Man."

20 "Assassination Records," 7–8.

21 "Organized Crime and Use of Violence, Hearings, Part 2" (Washington, DC: US Congress, May 1980), 400–406, https://www.ojp.gov/pdffiles1/Digitization/72649NCJRS.pdf.

22 Sally Bixby Defty, "Museum Theft Suspect Killed," *St. Louis Post-Dispatch*, June 18, 1978.

23 Defty, "Suspect Killed."

24 Defty, "Suspect Killed."

25 Sally Bixby Defty, "Ex-St. Louisan Is Questioned in Art Theft," *St. Louis Post-Dispatch*, January 24, 1979.

26 "Classified Ad: Antiques and Arts," *Chicago Tribune*, January 27–29, 1978, https://www.newspapers.com/image/386220015.

27   "Classified Ad: Antiques and Arts," *Chicago Tribune,* February 18, 1978, https://www.newspapers.com/image/386388065.

28   "Assassination Records," 7–8.

29   "Investigation of the Assassination of Martin Luther King, Jr.," vol. 7 (Washington, DC: US Government, 1979), 232, https://books.google.com/books?id=SW-z6uUxyd8C&pg.

30   "Martin Luther King," 235.

31   "Martin Luther King," 293–298.

32   Jo Mannies, "Charges House Panel Hired Ray Case Spy," *St. Louis Post-Dispatch,* August 8, 1978.

33   "Conclusions" in *Final Report of the Select Committee on the Assassination of Martin Luther King, Jr.* (Washington, DC: US Government, 1979), 371–374, https://books.google.com/books?id=XKA7AQAAMAAJ.

Chapter 10. The Pro vs. the Amateur

1   Sarah Bochicchio, "The Rothko Effect: Why Does Art Move Us?" *Phllips,* April 15, 2021, https://www.phillips.com/article/72737375/the-rothko-effect-why-does-art-move-us-twentieth-century-contemporary-art-london.

2   M.R.R. "A Group of Studies," *Bulletin of the City Art Museum of St. Louis,* no. 4 (October 1934), 49–50, http://www.jstor.org/stable/40714231.

3   James Elkins, *Pictures and Tears* (New York: Routledge, 2001), 162–165.

Chapter 11. Where Art Thou, Picasso?

1   Russell Targ, *The Reality of ESP: A Physicist's Proof of Psychic Phenomena* (Wheaton, IL: Quest Books, Theosophical Publishing House, 2012).

2   Fernande Olivier, Marilyn McCully, and John Richardson, *Loving Picasso: The Private Journal of Fernande Olivier* (New York: Harry N. Abrams, 2001).

3   Gabrielle C. Wilson and Yael M. Weitz, "In Review: Art Disputes in USA," *Lexology* (Herrick Feinstein LLP, January 17, 2021), https://www.lexology.com/library/detail.aspx?g=6f178693-7125-4b0f-a24b-dc10092b6e15.

4   John Henry Merryman, "The Good Faith Acquisition of Stolen Art" (October 29, 2007). Stanford Public Law Working Paper No. 1025515, https://ssrn.com/abstract=1025515.

About the Author

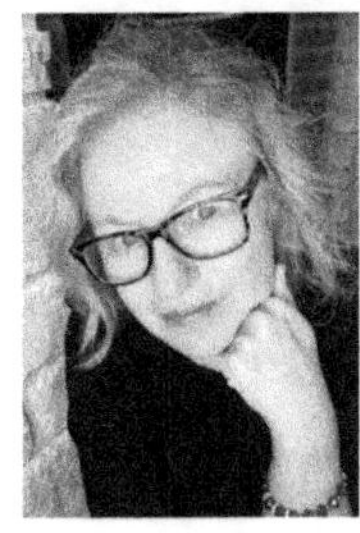

C. Joan Baker was born and raised in North St. Louis City, MO. Her curiosity and willingness to dive deeply into new interests were the common denominators that launched a successful business career and her first book, *Chasing Picasso*.

She broke the glass ceiling on more than one occasion and jokingly claimed she has the emotional scars to prove it. Her thirty-year gig that included research and writing proved to be an asset when she exchanged her corporate suit for fuzzy slippers and pj's (her most productive writing attire).

If you enjoyed the book, please leave a review online with the retailer or through the author's website, cjoanbaker.com.

Help the author spread the word about the missing Picasso! If you have information on the missing painting please submit the lead directly at cjoanbaker.com.

www.ingramcontent.com/pod-product-compliance
Lightning Source LLC
Chambersburg PA
CBHW071507140726
47997CB00005B/1891